# it's Me!

*Discovering the Self Within*

# it's Me!

*Discovering the Self Within*

Col R Suresh (retd)
Janani Suresh

PENTAGON PRESS LLP

First published in 2023 by
PENTAGON PRESS LLP
206, Peacock Lane, Shahpur Jat
New Delhi-110049, India
Contact: 011-64706243

Typeset in Palatino, 11 Point
Design & Layout: BALRAM DESANI
Printed by Aegean Offset Printers, Greater Noida, U.P.

ISBN: 978-93-90095-86-5 (HB)



**www.pentagonpress.in**

*We dedicate this book to our daughter and son-in-law with the aspiration that they bring up their children well, who achieve academic excellence, are emotionally and socially balanced as well as spiritually elevated.*

# CONTENTS

# FOREWORD

With great happiness, I am writing the foreword for this book, *"It's Me! Discovering the Self Within"* by Col R Suresh and his wife Mrs Janani Suresh.

The importance of discovering the self within and the significance of realizing that I am in charge of my life, all my thoughts, words and deeds and that no external factor can be held responsible for them is the primary aim of this book. At a time when there is a tendency to look for someone or something outside of us on which to pin the blame, this book comes as a reminder that I must first look inwards. This will make ME do what is required in the existing circumstances—to find a way instead of either giving excuses or grounds for not being able to do what has to be done.

Written in an easy, narrative style, touching upon a number of important issues which affect all of us in our day-to-day life, the book is a good guide for all those who wonder what to do when they feel they are at the crossroads of life. This book is recommended for all, not only to enjoy but also to learn and grow to become better human beings.

Happiness lies within us.

Wish you all a happy discovery.

Sadhu Apurvamunidas.

Pujya Apurvamuni Swami
*BAPS, Rajkot*

# MESSAGE

The book, *"It's me! Discovering the Self Within"* by Col R Suresh, SVP Admin, Marwadi University, Rajkot, and his spouse, Mrs Janani Suresh, reminds us of our forgotten core values that are the cornerstone for us to remain compassionate. It brings out the importance of always staying in touch with ourselves and to search for answers within ourselves instead of outside. The present day world has become very fast and does not have sufficient time. So, this book comes as a refreshing breeze where we are asked to find time for and meaning in relationships, understand the power of the mind and realize the value of becoming contributing members of society. This book is an amazing source of inspiration for all readers.

At the time when most of the universities are revising their curriculum in accordance with NEP 2020 and when the UGC has advised all of them to start foundation courses on human values and professional ethics at the undergraduate level as well as an advanced course for post-graduate students, this book is a good supplement to read and discover oneself. Ultimately, what we are looking for is not knowledge or experience alone but the way we use them and put what we have learnt into practice to add value to our society.

My personal favourite article from this book is 'Positive Psychology (Finding Happiness within)'. Happiness is the reflection of a positive state of mind and promotes a healthy lifestyle by reducing stress and blood pressure, improves our immune system, enables better sleep, and helps ease anxiety and depression. It has also been observed that cheerful people are more successful in various life areas like family, marriage, comradeship, earnings, professional work performance, etc. Hence it is very important for an individual to find happiness within and keep going.

Being an academician, I also highly encourage and appreciate another article based on Learning Beyond the Classroom which is wonderfully conveyed by the authors with the example of utilising the three H's, i.e. Head, Heart, and Hands in learning. A student has to develop additional skills in order to meet the expectations of a challenging world outside the institution and apply the knowledge gained through education in real-life practical situations. These skills may be in terms of practical knowledge of machines or relevant tools, sports, social or cultural, new language, emotional intelligence, effective communication, etc. As rightly said by Einstein, "Education is not the learning of facts, but the training of the mind to think."

While talking about universal human values, what is more important is not just reading or speaking about values but internalizing them in oneself and discovering the bliss within. This book, *'It's Me'* is written in a flowing style, easy to read and absorb. It is worth reading and can change the quality of our life.

**Prof. (Dr.) Sandeep Sancheti**
*Provost, Vice-Chancellor*
*Marwadi University*

# MESSAGE

Since our formative years at the Sainik School, Amaravathinagar, from 1969 to 1975, Suresh, in addition to being a close friend, has been inspiring me to rise above my perceived shortcomings and become a better version of myself. He is a key factor in my being able to successfully qualify the selection process and join the National Defence Academy, Khadakwasla, where we both were squadron mates in the Foxtrot Squadron. On 'Passing Out' from the Indian Military Academy on 9 June 1979, Suresh was commissioned into the Jat Regiment and I joined the Rajput Regiment. A rare combination of physical toughness with intellectual acumen and unimpeachable integrity, Suresh has always led by example, shunning pomp and showmanship. In all areas of endeavour, he effected considerable value addition; his actions speak in command, staff and in instructional assignments. During the Kargil War, Col. Suresh led his troops in a daring daylight attack which resulted in the capture of a key enemy occupied feature.

After retiring from the Army, Suresh continued to work with organizations striving to empower the young generation and subsequently joined the Marwari University at Rajkot as the SVP Administration. When the COVID-19 pandemic paralysed normal functioning globally, educational institutions were among the worst affected. More than the visible destructive effects of the pandemic, the overwhelming sense of despair, gloom and hopelessness led to depression and a sense of despondency which threatened to cause exponential damage many times in excess of those affected directly by the scourge. To combat that threat, Suresh along with his equally courageous and committed team mate, Mrs. Janani Suresh, authored a series of thirty-one inspiring and motivational articles in the University journal. Each of them, written in lucid, easy-to-comprehend prose, carries very powerful life messages addressing a particular area of concern. Along with quotations by great personalities, and proven examples of success, the articles inspire the reader to focus on positivity and take concrete, tangible steps to overcome each problem, judiciously avoiding self-created pitfalls caused by a negative mindset. Each of the thirty-one topics emphasises the power of every individual to overcome adverse situations by drawing upon the amazing power of the mind.

I am glad that Suresh has acceded to the earnest request by the staff and students who were inspired by these messages, and compiled the articles in a book which will enable them to be accessed by a larger reader base. Each of these topics deserves to be read deliberately and the messages internalised and implemented with full sincerity to change gears and zoom ahead in life.

**Col K K Arun, SM (retd)**
*24th Battalion, The RAJPUT Regiment*

# ACKNOWLEDGEMENTS

We know that no propellant can take off without an igniter. There are many who were involved in making this book see print form and my heartfelt gratitude to each one of them.

I am grateful to Dr Rajkumar for instilling the thought of publishing the monthly articles as a book for wider readership. He sowed the seed which has now bloomed into a full-fledged book. I am thankful to Dr Poorna Chandra Reddy Alla for encouraging me in my endeavour.

My colleague, Dr Bijay Bhujbal, was responsible for designing the cover page and making it relevant and meaningful and my special thanks are due to him. I must make a special mention of Mr Abhay Chauhan, my friend, who was a great support during the entire course of my work.

A big thank to Mr Balram Desani who gave feedback, set the type and did the formatting to make it appealing.

I am thankful to my NDA buddies Col K K Arun and General Anil Sengar for their unstinted moral support and for ensuring I went ahead with the project.

I must also place on record my gratitude to Mr Rajan Arya,

Pentagon Press LLP who went out of his way to help my debut venture see light.

I am especially indebted to the management of Marwadi University, the Provost, faculty, staff and my entire admin team for their wholehearted support and cooperation.

There are many more well wishers who were instrumental in breaking my inertia in bringing this book out for the happy reading of all and I owe them all my deep thanks.

Finally, but not the least, I am grateful to God for everything and my parents for educating me and inculcating ethical values in me.

# PREFACE

The monthly bulletin of the organization I work for included an article in every issue which would touch upon some important aspect of our day-to-day life. The articles covered health, hygiene, behaviour, leadership and so on. What started as articles for the monthly bulletin has now come out as a book, *"IT'S ME!"* our debut venture, which is a joint effort by my wife, Janani Suresh and me. She was the one who would critically read, add value and shape the material in the existing form. She stood by my side as co-author to endeavour to make the articles relevant and with something worthwhile to carry home.

It was essentially done to share my experiences of what I have learnt over the years as an individual and also from my profession as an Army officer. I was happy to see that the articles touched a chord in all those who read them. It was only recently that some of our well-wishers suggested that we compile the various articles in book form. So, we have tried to put together the articles with a similar theme under one main subject though written at different times.

The book titled, *'IT'S MĖ!'* refers to discovering the self within. Every day we see or hear different things or interact with different people and each transaction becomes a learning occasion. However, seldom do we realize that it is only the change that we bring in ourselves which takes us to the next level of happiness, contentment and accomplishment. This book aims for introspection and self-transformation to make us fit in well with the environment and at the same time remain true to ourselves too. So, it is not a book to be read in a hurry but to be read at a relaxed pace, introspected upon, and internalized.

The cover of the book, conceived and designed by my friend, Dr Bijay Bhujabal, has five colours. In his words, "The olive green stands for your experience as a soldier, the grey exemplifies executive sophistication as an able administrator and the pink represents the pink of health and happiness as can be seen from your articles on physical, mental, psychological and spiritual well being which come from your interest and study of subjects in counselling, psychology, management, leadership and administration. The fourth colour, maroon embodies sacrifice and the fifth one, yellow letters in the centre is to draw attention. It signifies the light which emanates from within us and is the central life force that connects us with this world. It stands for sanctity, positive vibes, optimism, energy, joy, and happiness."

Many of the articles in this compilation were written at different times in 2020 and 2021, the two years which have been totally unlike any in the known past. While the content of some of the articles might be related to the new world situation created by and during the pandemic, the lessons learnt from them will definitely be useful in the future too and have a far-reaching impact on the way we think and grow.

This book has been packed in six chapters. Though clubbed under different headings for ease of identification, the articles are individual pieces and they could be read in any order, not necessarily sequentially. The first chapter addresses some important behavioural skills, the second deals with forgotten soft skills which were rekindled by the COVID waves, the third touches upon the aspects of true education and developing one's memory, the fourth touches upon the leadership traits picked up during my time in Olive Greens which I consider are essential, the fifth chapter talks of life skills learnt from our experiences and the final chapter concludes with some important aspects on self development. The aim of these articles is to awaken that something within us which will help us discover our core values, become better human beings and more productive people in society. Learning not only includes information collection and knowledge but something more—a growth not only in the intelligence quotient but also in sociability, adaptability, emotional stability and finally, in finding true contentment.

Every day, life gives us all many opportunities to observe and learn and one of the lessons learnt during the pandemic is expressed beautifully in this quote, "Trust the Wait. Embrace the Uncertainty. Enjoy the beauty of Becoming. When nothing is certain, anything is possible."

Leaving you to ponder over these words as you step into the book, "IT'S ME!"—It is always me.

# CHAPTER I

# I, ME, MYSELF

## 1.1 Positive Psychology

### *My Happiness*

We find some people are always happy and cheerful, some are always experiencing problems, some always remain introverts without appreciating what goes on around them, and some are unhappy as things keep going wrong for them. Why is this so? It is believed that the answer actually lies within oneself and depends on the way one looks at things. To see a thing as big or small, one as rich or poor, as healthy or weak, or as good or bad, lucky or unlucky is all one's perception.

If we look at the truth about happiness and also the ever-fading and impermanent emotions and feelings, we will realize that it is these emotions and feelings that take us through a state of happiness, sadness, depression, suffering or great sense of achievement. Let us take one example, say Happiness, for our understanding.

Happiness is a state, an outcome of a particular feeling. Happiness is a good state and all living beings have evolved to pursue a signal that needs to be satisfied. So, the signal of happiness is from the state of mind we have identified for ourselves. Also, from the area we try to explore—the bad side or the good side of things.

Someone has said, "We are happy when we are healthy, well fed, comfortable, safe, prosperous, knowledgeable, respected, and loved." However, it is not so simple because in spite of all these things being available, many are not happy. In fact, a survey of the level of happiness shows that the average level of happiness varies from region to region. This is due to the conditions of environment/circumstances people live in and the Darwinian theory of natural selection. So, an entire community evolves and generally has similar traits. However, it is individually possible to improve our level of happiness by being consciously aware of our feelings and emotions and working on them.

One has to realize an interesting phenomenon about an individual's state of mind—it is never permanent and never at rest. If we are happy today, the same will become irrelevant/weak/fade away with time and situation. It may be because our base level of happiness has gone up or we have adapted to the situation that it no more gives the required signal to our brain or we have become immune to the happiness due to continuous repetitions of the same or similar situations.

So, let us see some facts about happiness.

### *a) Happiness Set Point*

The way we appreciate certain things, the amount of happiness we exhibit and how events affect us and how well we adapt and get used to them is a set point which is heritable and the range is genetically fixed. The level of happiness does not change naturally or on its own (as much as we think). In fact it is not so much what happens to us that determines how happy we are, rather, it is how we perceive it. The mind is its own place and in itself, can make a heaven of hell or a hell of heaven. Shakespeare has said, "There is nothing good or bad but what thinking make it so."

### *b) Happiness is Relative*

You give a person, "A," Rs. 50,000 and person "B" Rs. 20,000; "A" is very happy but, when you give Rs. 50,000to "A" and Rs. 80,000 to "B", "A" is very unhappy. So it is not the 50,000 that gives happiness, but the perception that makes us happy or sad. Our happiness is not from what we achieve or are blessed with but from the relative perceptions that we make in our mind. When I go to a village and interact with the underprivileged people there, I feel that I am more blessed than they are but, at the same time, in the company of great achievers, I feel small and inadequate. In fact, some high-average people get an inferiority complex when in the company of very intelligent people. You might have heard of some IITians getting depressed and committing suicide. One has to be conscious of the fact that it is the mind working in the wrong direction. The student was happy when he cracked JEE and got into the elite crowd but reached a state of depression when he found himself low in comparison to his intelligent peers. It can be compared to the dots placed close together on elastic tape. When stretched, the distance between them suddenly increases; in the same way, when all the highly intelligent students join IIT, the differences are not noticeable, but when stretched to their capacity, the differences show up and the person at the lower end is not able to accept the fact that he is not the best.

### *c) Happiness is Temporary*

Events make us happy or sad but the events do not last for

ever. They fade away. In fact, some events that take us to the extreme become meaningless with the passage of time. So why get affected by them? If we look inside ourselves, we will find that the events themselves do not give happiness, but it is the way we look at the event that gives the signal of happiness. Remember that the same event does not give the same level of happiness to two different persons or at two different times to the same person. A person got the news that he had won the jackpot in a lottery. Even before he collected the prize, he was in the seventh heaven as his mind had perceived so many wonderful things. However, when he went to collect the reward, he was told that it was a misprint. As he did not get the prize, he became extremely dejected. Before the news and after the news, at both times, he did not get the lottery jackpot amount, but the feelings and emotions attached to the event triggered his happiness and disappointment.

So, the way to be happy is to be composed while looking at things, that is, to train to see the environment with positivity and without any attachment, to accept and let go, with the self not clinging to these temporary and fading emotions and feelings.

A positive outlook will reinforce our positive energy and cause the ones which do not contribute to our good to fade away. A simple theory of Operant Conditioning works. Events generate thoughts in the mind, thoughts convert to action and actions become a habit. So, let us feed in positive thoughts and understand the reality. The mind never generates thoughts when busy with the present —here and now. Thoughts come from somewhere else to fill our mind if empty. So let us keep our mind full with actions and positive inputs. Happiness will be the outcome. In fact it will be bliss. We would have experienced it many times when we were fully involved in some work. We would not have even felt the passing of time during that blissful experience. Then why not fill the mind with positive thoughts and have the benefit of happiness by being with the present?

Some more truths about feeling good.

### *a) The End matters*

Whatever we go through, if the outcome or the final result is good, we carry home all happiness; however, if we start well but end on a bad note, the scar remains throughout. So, the effort put in should be commensurate with the end desired. We should try to ensure that our entire journey ends on a positive note by putting our heart and soul in whatever we do. Then, our life will be happy. In fact, in work places, HR heads and bosses ensure that the farewell is always good so that positive memories of the parting make the employee speak highly of the system. After all, he is another ambassador for the organization.

### *b) Equanimity and Optimism*

Positive psychology refers to training ourselves to understand what makes us happy. Does the event actually make us happy or the way we perceive it? A simple way to be happy is to show poise or equanimity with negative feelings (ego, selfishness, anger, fear, lust, worry, suspicion, jealousy, etc.) removed from us. With an accommodating attitude, we reach the next level to understand that more than half of the cause of our feelings is we ourselves and not external factors. Positive Thoughts, Balanced Outlook and Optimism are the key to Happiness.

Finally, it is we who are responsible for our happiness and no one else. While half our thinking is based on heredity, we are responsible for the other half—we can change it by our positive attitude, compassion, level-headedness, and optimism. We spend a lot of time to do well in our academic education, but hardly do we devote time to train our mind to be emotionally strong and develop emotional intelligence to perceive things and find happiness in all that we hear, see and do. Happiness is in everything, we have to learn to find it.

Happiness is a habit and we can practise it.

✧✧✧✧✧

## 1.2 My Choices/Experiences

### *Every Choice is Right*

Robert Frost's famous poem, "The Road Not Taken" speaks of the poet standing in the woods at the junction point where two roads diverge, and trying to make a choice on which one to take. He is confused as to which one to choose and finally decides on one of them.

Similarly, we too are faced with choices at every stage of life—and the decisions we take lead us in a particular direction. We make a particular choice based on some information or some intuitive feeling. There is no way of going back to that point in life again to have the same choices. One choice will lead us one way while the other a different way. The poet says that at a later stage in life he might regret the choice he made, but adds that the choice he took has made him what he is today. The important message that he conveys is that the choices we make have an impact on our future, our destiny.

However, I would like to touch upon a different aspect of the same theme on choices—that with time we will realize that no choice is right or wrong; it is only a matter of gaining a different set of experiences based on our choice. "Life is a journey with problems to solve, lessons to learn, but most of all, experiences to enjoy."

There are examples of so many people who became doctors or engineers or lawyers because of certain circumstances that pushed them into that position. However, when they were able to reason out for themselves, they changed their profession to follow their passion in music or fine arts. According to William Maphoto, "It is never too late to reconsider our choices." We have the right to change our minds and make a new choice at any point in our life. The earlier decision, probably taken by a parent, was not wrong. It must have been taken in their wisdom, for providing stability and status to their children but when the change was made, the person had gained from his knowledge in a different field as every experience makes one grow. "Every new experience brings its own maturity and a greater clarity of vision."

There is a story which brings this out—to go beyond the right and wrong because Life has a lot more to teach us.

There were five men who were walking through a huge forest and suddenly they realized they were hopelessly lost. Each suggested a different route which the others were not ready to agree to. So, they decided to part ways and take the path of their choice. The first man said he was going to follow his intuition that going to the left was the best option. The second decided to go to the right as he had a strong feeling it was the way out. The third person believed that going back on the path they had come would be the safest route to take.

The fourth member scoffed at the other three and announced that they were actually on the right track and so he would go straight on in the same direction. The fifth man did not say anything then as he had not decided on anything yet.

After the four men took to different directions they believed were correct—left, right, backward and straight ahead, the fifth man realized he was not sure which route to choose and felt he could take a better decision after climbing up a tall tree and seeing the world from there to get a better view.

In fact, he felt the others had not even stopped to consider the options and had just jumped into their decisions. He, on the other hand, was now going to make an informed decision based on what he could see from a height. He found the shortest route to a nearby village and reached there.

We realize one aspect from the fifth man's way of working —of pausing, thinking, and then taking action. Rising above a situation gives us a larger picture and we do not miss the wood for the trees. Distancing one self and gaining perspective is a valuable lesson for life

The fifth man was proud of himself, and felt that the others were not as smart as he was. He felt he had taken the right decision in climbing up the tree to look for a route whereas the others were wrong in rushing away in different directions.

However, life is not a situation where someone has to prove himself smarter than another person; in fact, it is a journey where one learns different things and gains different experiences based on the choices one makes. From one point of view, the fifth man was right but, from another perspective, so were the others.

Each had gained a different experience. Moreover, each had chosen his own path and the journey had enriched each one of them in a unique way. It is not a question of right or wrong, but gaining our own experience and finding our own path.

The man who went left had to go on a long and arduous path but he finally reached the town, tired but happy that he had made it and had also learnt to survive against all odds. The man who had turned towards the right had to fight a pack of wolves but it taught him how to endure in a jungle and had also given him a bundle of stories to narrate to his children back home! The man who went back on the route they had come along, met another group of hikers with whom he became friends and thus gained from his new and enlarged circle of associates; and the man who had gone straight ahead reached a farm where he was hosted by the family there for a couple of days before he left for his city. He enjoyed their hospitality and could unwind in new surroundings. Of course, the man who had climbed the tree had found the shortest route to a village. The journey had provided a new experience to each one in a special way. Each would have a different narrative to recount!

Every decision offers us new experiences and this makes us more mature, more human. We gain more wisdom which ultimately leads to our growth. People who have undergone more in life are more seasoned, so to say. Depending on how life has treated each person, some get hardened, some get bitter but some ripen well and use their life lessons to live more fulfilling lives and serve as guiding beacons for others because of their vast experience. Learning from such people adds to our own experience.

Blindly following another person without using our own common sense and discerning power is meaningless. It is said, 'Life is like an exam.' Many fail because they try to copy others not realizing that each one has a different question paper and each is answering a different test! We must learn to walk our own path while at the same time learn from the experiences of others. Experiencing everything firsthand is not necessary, we have the lessons learnt by others for our knowledge and that should add to our repertoire of understanding. We stand on the shoulders of those who have gone before us and their learning shows us the path we could choose. However, finally, the choice is ours and ours alone. We have no right to blame anyone for anything, as, even if we do what another wishes us to, the choice to follow that decision also, was only ours.

James Hauenstein states that we should not have any regrets in life because of the choices we make. Good or bad, they are a learning experience, to help us grow. The only regret in life, according to him, is to never make a choice at all. Making choices and taking decisions are very important in life. Actually, there are two primary choices—to accept conditions as they exist or accept responsibility for changing them. One is a passive approach, whereas the second is the kind where we take life head-on, as it comes and take charge of ourselves and our lives.

"It is my road and mine alone. Others may walk it with me, but no one can walk it for me." So, at the end of the day, I am responsible for my life, my choices, and my decisions.

We learn to make the 'right choices' after getting experience and we gain 'experience' only after making 'wrong choices'! So, let us learn from our experiences gained from the choices made by us. This makes us better equipped for life and also gives us a broader and more holistic view of life. Let us live our lives fully by enjoying what life offers, make the choices we think best at that point and keep moving ahead with confidence and contentment.

✧✧✧✧✧

## 1.3 The Seventh Man

### The Voice Within

All of us must have heard the story of the missing seventh man. The story goes like this—Seven friends were walking together and going to meet their guru. They stopped for a dip in a wayside river. When they had all bathed, one of them suddenly said, "One of us is missing!" When the others expressed shock, he counted out loudly for them,— one, two, three, four, five, and six. All gasped in disbelief. The others too tried out one by one but they also could count only six. They looked into the distance along the length of the river, searching for the missing seventh friend. Not able to find anyone, they started crying loudly, lamenting for their friend who they presumed had been carried away by the current. They were sad, angry, bewildered, confused and feeling miserable. Luckily for them, a man was passing by. He saw their forlorn condition and enquired empathetically. They explained the situation to him. He counted them and found that all seven were present! He realized he was speaking to a bunch of fools and understood they had all counted only the others, not themselves! He told them that he would produce the seventh person and they should reward him if he could do it. So, he tapped on the first man's hand, who then said, "ONE." Similarly came TWO, then THREE, followed by FOUR, FIVE, SIX, and finally, SEVEN! They were overjoyed that the missing seventh friend had been found and gave the clever man some money for helping them and then proceeded joyfully to the guru's place, not even realizing the mistake they had made.

This is a story we have all read or heard and laughed over the foolishness of the men. Actually, there is a deeper meaning to this childish story which many of us may not be aware of. When the men in the story forgot to count themselves, it actually refers to the conscience. Like, when we make a mistake and we look over our shoulders to see if anybody has observed it, we have forgotten ourselves! Our own conscience has seen us and we know we have made a mistake. Conscience is a man's compass. A guru once gives his students a mango each and tells them to eat it secretly, without being seen by anyone else. All of them eat their mangoes, hiding in various places but, one shishya (disciple) brings it back and says he was not able to do it as there were two people seeing what he was doing at all times. They were his conscience and the all-pervading Universal God!

So, even if no one else sees us, the awareness of these two is sufficient to ensure we do not go astray. In order to be able to sleep peacefully at night, we should listen to our inner voice which is essentially a drop of the main ocean. George Washington urges "Labour to keep alive in your breast that little spark of celestial fire called conscience." To stay on the right track, to do our assigned work without supervision and not to give in to temptation when no one else is around is possible only when we remember that our conscience is always seeing us. The feeling of guilt on committing a mistake cannot be forgotten or washed away or brushed aside. It will keep gnawing a person from within. Sophocles is so right when he says that there is no witness so terrible and no accuser as powerful as the conscience which dwells within us. Probably, one way of atonement is to open ourselves up to someone we can trust and share with them what is eating us from within. This is a kind of expression of our remorse for the act and seeking forgiveness from God. It will at least release bottled-up feelings.

In the story of the *Mahabharata*, which can be considered as a metaphor for all our qualities, good and bad, the youngest son of Dhritharashtra, Yuyutsu, is considered to be the inner voice, the voice of conscience. When, on the orders of Duryodhana, Dushasana tries to disrobe Draupadi, the only person who speaks up against it is Yuyutsu. All the others, including the elders in the court, are under various levels of delusion and compulsions and self-made conditions and do not speak up in spite of knowing that the act is wrong and condemnable. They maintain an ominous silence which makes them part of the crime. Acts of omission are as bad as acts of commission which is why even all the learned and revered seniors in the court are killed in the war for supporting the person doing wrong, not wantonly, but for actually not having the courage to stop the wrong act. Yuyutsu alone speaks up, but he is brushed aside by his eldest brother, Duryodhana, and so he leaves the court, never to return. It is symbolic of killing the conscience, which once smothered will rarely be able to raise its head again. We see this in hardened criminals and terrorists who without any qualms are able to take someone's life. In the initial stages, probably their conscience would have pricked them and given them sleepless nights, but by ignoring and suppressing their inner voices, or by justifying their action, they were able to continue without being affected by it—and then, the voice stops speaking.

So, when we do any action, we have to see if we ourselves are content and satisfied, that is, is our conscience happy with it or whether we are ignoring the voice within for the sake of our work/money—whether we are compromising in some way or are able to stand up for what is right by not stifling our inner voice. We may or may not remain in the same job for ever, but we have to live with our conscience always and there is no way of escaping from the inner voice. When a person speaks of job satisfaction, it is this aspect which is the actual criterion. He is able to live with himself peacefully.

Teaching children to listen to and follow their inner voice is important, it empowers them. In the book *"You Can Win"* by Shiv Khera, the author brings out the same aspect of the conscience, but, puts it across in a different way. He calls it the Mama test and the Baba test. The first one directs us to think of our mother (mama) before doing an act which is morally wrong. "Will my mother be proud of me if I do this or, will she have to hang her head in shame?" That will ensure there is no irrational desire to indulge in. The second one—

Baba test—is to think of our children. When they come to know what their mother or father has done will they look up to us as role models or feel like avoiding us and hiding the fact from their peers that we are their parents? If these two tests can be carried out successfully, we will always be in consonance with our conscience and never regret any action in life. In fact, we must never do an action which will lower us in our own eyes—rather, we must always set high standards for ourselves and strive to reach them.

As Harper Lee puts it, "Before I can live with other folks, I've got to live with myself. The one thing that doesn't abide by majority rule is a person's conscience."

*"The Voice*

*There is a voice inside of you That whispers all day long, "I feel this is right for me,*

*I know that this is wrong."*

*No teacher, preacher, parent, friend Or wise man can decide*

*What's right for you—just listen to The voice that speaks inside."*

**—Shel Silverstein**

✧✧✧✧✧

## *1.4 My Values*

### *The Need of the Hour*

It is a big bad world out there. Corruption reigns supreme. It is rightly said, "Power corrupts and absolute power corrupts absolutely." Whether it is politics or any other field, there is an ulterior motive in everything. Everyone feels that only if I have bigger and better and costlier stuff, then I am better than the other person. At the drop of a hat, we take offence; even countries do not mind destroying property, lives and the environment and no one is able to stop the destruction taking place. Ego clashes both at individual and international levels are on the rise and seem set to take mankind to the brink of total ruin.

In India too, a sea change is taking place. Our traditional food, language, culture, dress, habits, work culture, and festivals have almost changed. These days we celebrate Valentine's Day, Fathers' Day and Mothers' Day which have the least connection to our way of life. Malls have opened up everywhere. I may be in any part of the country, but I have the same branded stuff and it is the same throughout the nation, rather, the world. There is nothing unique which makes each state or city different and special. We used to celebrate unity in diversity, but now, there seems to be a kind of uniformity rather than distinctiveness. That is how MNCs have literally swept us off our feet. The East India Company came to trade and stayed on to rule. A similar insidious kind of invasion is taking place and we are not even aware of it! Pub culture has taken over and fast foods have an enticing as well as an addicting quality which is undeniable and seem to have greater mass appeal than traditional foods.

People have become materialistic and everything seems to have a price. With the availability of information on everything under the sun on the net, nothing is sacred anymore. When I switch on the news on any TV channel or pick up the newspaper, the one thing that hits me first is the amount of wrong doings which have either become rampant or maybe, are the only items worth reporting—be it robbery or larceny or murder or arson or blackmailing or forgery or extortion or smuggling or assault or molestation or cyber crime, or scams of all kinds or crypto frauds or money laundering, the list is endless. Gun culture too has entered our shores.

Where are we heading? What has happened to our value system? Why are we moving towards the law of the Jungle? Are we leaving the world in a good state for the children of tomorrow? The present order of things seems to be a recipe for disaster.

There is a definite erosion of our values which we as a nation cherished, treasured and upheld. According to Christopher Kolade, "It is not enough if I stand for what is right, it is important to let people know what I stand for." That is how it was in our previous generations. There were very clear-cut VALUES as to what was right or wrong. There were no ambiguous signals and the next generation learnt right from wrong at a very early age. The entire society believed in and followed the same yardstick and we imbibed what we saw, heard and experienced all around us.

Then, with each generation (old to the present day), the rules started to change. Being bad, doing wrong and getting away with it became the new benchmark for measuring who was 'SMART'! Earlier, someone who was well groomed and spoke well was considered smart. That has changed. Movies too show cool, suave heroes who con people. Being 'goody-goody' did not make one look smart whereas being audacious did. To be judged better than the others, it was not necessary to be right as to be 'smart'—smart not to get caught, smart to pass on responsibility and smart not to volunteer when it did not benefit self. Breaking the rules became the norm rather than an exception. Being bad became the new good!

By advocating the wrong thing or, by not supporting the right thing, a very mistaken value has been given to this generation—the Gen Next. The signals sent by us to the present generation are conflicting. It somehow seems acceptable to cheat or lie if the situation demands it which causes dichotomy in our minds.

We are engulfed by corruption and yet, when someone does something good, the act stands out as a beacon for others. There is still goodness left in the world and it is the virtuous people who are taking the world forward. "Everything I do right now ripples outward and affects everyone." Every selfless act, justice, generosity and philanthropy stands out as an example for people to follow. For every act of crime, there are many more acts of honesty and righteousness. However, there is a tendency to highlight the transgressions rather than acts of truthfulness and uprightness. Though it is necessary for the sake of correction and learning, it should not be over-emphasized as that has an unfavourable impact on the mind. All of us should instead throw light more often on all the good that happens to spread positive vibrations.

To bring back the VALUE SYSTEM into our lives and into the lives of the torchbearers for the coming generations, we ourselves should always send the right signals to them. We should uphold right values and listen to our conscience. That requires moral courage, strength of conviction and belief in oneself. WE ARE FIRST AND FOREMOST ANSWERABLE TO OURSELVES.

People learn not so much from what we say to them but from what we do. Today's generation is exposed to so much around them; they are influenced not only by their parents but also by their peers and media and movies that they prefer to follow the 'easy' path rather than the right one. So, to be able to have an impact on the new generation, not only should we do right but also be seen doing right and spend time talking to them about it.

Assignments and projects for the young, where they themselves discover the value of values will have greater value. Involving all in awareness programmes, seminars, talks, discussions, debates, symposiums and street plays on morals and ethics would be a great idea. If someone takes the wrong track, punishment may not be the best deterrent. The realization should come from within. So, talking, counselling and discussing long-term consequences might have a better outcome. For the younger lot, it could be included as a subject in their curriculum.

What seemed effortless and automatic to most people for earlier generations has now become a matter of choice for the present-day millennials. So, repeated exposure to what is right, maximum experience with its positive effects and the greatest efforts to teach the superiority of good over bad will be obligatory. It is everyone's responsibility to do this. Albert Einstein says, "Try not to become a man of success, but rather try to become a man of value." Values should be inculcated in them from the seed itself so that we create a generation with High Values and Principles for, after all, it is CHARACTER that is the mark of a man. With that, we can be satisfied and feel fulfilled that we have done our duty as good human beings, elders, parents, teachers and well-wishers for the successors of tomorrow's world.

✧✧✧✧✧

## *1.5 My Mind Set and Attitude*

### *Run Rajkot Run*

Dear folks! Let me take you on an exciting journey! It is 5 am of Sunday, 29 December 2019. The atmosphere is windy and very cold. The temperature is hovering between 11 and 12 degrees Celsius! The whooshing chill breeze is freezing the already icy hands and face—the only exposed parts. We are at Rajkot Race Course grounds. No one in his/her right mind would have ventured out on an unearthly cold December morning, that too, on a Sunday! However, be ready to be surprised—when I reached at 4.45 am, the race course was already alive and teeming with a humongous crowd! I discovered there were 35,000-plus participants, almost touching 37,000! It looked like most Rajkotians preferred to be out in the open in their orange and white or grey T shirts! What an involved lot, I thought. Each of them had come with the intention of becoming fit—a fit Rajkot, for a fit, vibrant Gujarat, for a fit, robust India!

The 29th of December, 2019 was the day for all Rajkotians to run—It was the day of the half marathon—a 21-km run, the10-km challenge run and the 5-km fun run. Moreover, it was for a noble cause—to start a diabetic centre in Rajkot—something worthwhile for the people of the city.

The Race Course ground is spacious and the organizers—the Rotary Club of Rajkot along with many generous sponsors and partners had made excellent arrangements. Cars and buses were parked outside conveniently with ample moving space between them. There were enclosures for viewers, guests, and sponsors. The stage had a huge display screen showing live footage of the entire Race Course and happenings of this mega event. The anchor made the environment lively and connected with the people with ease. The young and enthusiastic volunteers went around in those early morning hours to help people in the biting cold which was really heart-warming to experience. To enliven the early morning hours and to warm the chilled soles, there were young zumba dancers jiving and jumping to metallic tunes. The music was energizing, vitalizing, and motivating everyone to jump or dance.

Not only in response to the playing of peppy tunes but also to keep the heart pumping and blood circulating quickly and to warm the freezing limbs, everyone was literally on their toes! Lights were flashing, colours changing, and the sound systems were adding to the enjoyment.

The Honourable Chief Minister of Gujarat, Shri Vijaybhai Rupani, too made it a point to come with his retinue to motivate the runners and he flagged off the 21-km run after an address. Tricoloured balloons were released into the sky to mark the moment. He waved to the enthusiastic runners to boost their morale and stayed on to flag-off the 10-km and 5-km runs.

It was all a matter of a great attitude and mindset that so many were out to challenge themselves. They were out to push their limits, to try and raise the bar for themselves. They were not competing with anyone; it was their own stamina, willpower, and fitness levels they were testing. They were out to break their own previous timings. The first-timers were out to assess their mettle, grit, determination, and spirit. All the participants were doing so of their own free will. They had to pay to register and instead of asking "What is there in it for me?", or, "Why should I pay and waste my Sunday?" they were bubbling with excitement to start running! It was because they either wanted to experience the marathon or they wanted to contribute to a worthwhile cause or, most probably, both. Of the 37,000 participants, many would have been first time-runners and the excitement was palpable throughout the morning.

At regular intervals in the route, there were stalls with water and refreshments. In addition, there were cheer girls to ensure one did not get tired! There were dancers, not only on the main stage where they had performed the zumba, but also all along the entire way, to add to the joie-de-vivre. They were performing the double role of entertaining and encouraging. Their presence was like being out in a fete, a gala carnival or on a celebration tour. The pressure of the run did not exist at all; it was like moving from one stall to another and finishing the run without even realizing it!

So, attitude makes a lot of difference. It might be just a run, but so much preparation had gone into it—behind the stage as it were—for the organizers—planning well ahead, putting up hoardings, registering the participants, getting the Race Course ground shipshape, setting of water points and health drinks en route, stalls for refreshments after the run, getting doctors and medical helpers and physiotherapists to support and aid those in need, marking the route for the various runs, getting people to sponsor, sending out invitations, sending messages to participants, giving their bib numbers, giving them sports kits, the bib number card with a digital chip affixed—the list is endless. Similarly, for the runners, it was their attitude that made all the difference. Firstly getting mentally prepared for the run, working to get themselves ready for it, practising days on end, sacrificing so many things to be ready for the occasion, paying and registering and then finally realizing that the die had been cast and now there was no turning back, no more internal debating on whether or not to participate! The date of registration was open till 15 December; after that date, those who had given their names would ensure they practised hard to make up for the lost time!

The attitude of runners and organizers was definitely important to ensure the grand success of the event. The viewers, who had come to cheer their family and friends and volunteers who came to be a part of the great experience, too, had the right attitude. Here, what needs special mention is a senior citizen who has been at marathons for years. He is a 70+ young gentleman who was participating for the 56th time! He had also joined the 50-km cyclathon earlier. Such people are real inspirations for others. Similarly, one must applaud the first-timers, who came up strong to participate, to overcome their own inertia, to build up their mental readiness for it, to develop stamina through practice and finally to complete whichever run they opted for, which is no mean achievement. I am sure many more Rajkotians would have found encouragement to participate in similar runs in coming years.

If our attitude is right, we will succeed. "My goal is not to be better than anyone else, but to be better than I used to be." This is true not only for running in the marathon, but for all aspects of life. After all, it is said, "It is our Attitude, more than Aptitude that will determine our Altitude."

✧✧✧✧✧

## *1.6 Virtual Emotion*

### *Does it Cater to Human Needs?*

About 40 years ago, I was a young captain in the Army, commanding an infantry company of approximately 150 army men, at heights of more than 12,000 feet and our company pay day is still fresh in my memory to this day. It used to be called 'pay parade'. It was held on the 1st of every month when the soldiers' salary was distributed in person.

The event involved assembling all the soldiers from their respective posts located far away at the HQ to collect their salaries. It used to be at a ground where the company commander would be seated at the centre of the table with the company subedar, senior JCOs, accounts clerk and pay NCO, all seated around him. The money and all the required papers for the soldiers would be kept on the table.

The parade would start at 8 a.m. and would continue till dinner time culminating in the favourite 'liquor parade' when the soldiers would take their two pegs of rum, snacks and special dinner, the 'bara khana' where the soldiers, the company commander, and the JCOs and NCOs would all dine together. It was a day that all would look forward to. It was not only a day when the soldiers would receive their pay, it was also a day when all the company men would meet and greet each other at a common place.

During the course of the pay distribution, soldiers would meet their friends, other soldiers from their village, their colleagues, batch mates and leaders and discuss everything under the sun. It was the time to again get connected almost after a month doing their duty at far flung posts; the occasion was actually a celebration of getting together!

Each soldier would spend at least 10 to 15 minutes with me while collecting his hard-earned small salary. It was all in cash those days. Some would opt for a lesser amount as they planned to go home on leave the next month when they would prefer to take the balance. Each interaction was a real emotional connection. He would take time to narrate his experiences during his duty and at his post. The soldier would share all his feelings and the talk would go beyond the professional—the issues he had faced, into his personal life, his health, his ambitions, his family and all aspects of concern and fun.

There could be a sudden burst of sorrow in the air or a volley of slang with happiness and joy all around, a request for a confidential personal meeting or counselling or a long silence conveying many unsaid emotions. I had to show empathy, give a patient hearing and provide advice or help. Solutions were found instantaneously and the team would feel comfortable and bonding would be much beyond professional—junior to boss. These were real. The soldier knew he could bank on you and that you were genuinely concerned in his welfare. Many times, matters were resolved without speaking or writing. Just a look would convey that I had understood what he wanted and the solution would be accepted without long-winded procedures and mail directions or confirmations. Everyone would work to connect better, build a team with an esprit de corps (a feeling of pride and mutual loyalty shared by the members of a group) and have a real bonding and not a virtual one.

All these types of events have gone with time—Gone with the Wind. Today, salary is disbursed through ECS online. Many times the soldier joins duty and leaves without meeting his company commander or other men of his company even once. Most communications are virtual...telephone, mobile, whatsApp or mail. You are totally connected with the job in hand but all the aspects of sharing, connecting, empathy and true communications are lost. You are connected, but not emotionally. You might have gained time but in reality you have lost the main thing—the basic requirement of social bonding and real-time emotional connect.

The story goes that an old man was walking to the bank once to collect his money. Someone asked him, "Why don't you go to the nearest ATM? Wouldn't that be faster?" The man said, "Does the ATM talk? And, I am in no hurry. I have all the time in the world. I would like to meet the bank staff, whom I know, and who know me for years—in fact since this branch opened some thirty years ago! Some time spent with them makes me feel good. My friends will also come today and we will catch up with each other. We look forward to these occasions." How true and touching.

Even at home, how much time do we spend together speaking with one another? It is common to see the family either sitting in different rooms with their laptops or mobiles or sometimes in the same room, but each with his or her mobile. There is no bonding—each one is busy with his work or enjoying a joke by himself. One forwards questions or information to the others and gets replies on the mobile! At the office too, we prefer to send an SMS/whatsApp message/mail rather than walk across to the next cabin and talk which is a million times better for connecting emotionally than all these virtual ones. It is so sad to see that humans are very busy running after possessions and profession leaving behind the real emotional connect and replacing it with a virtual one thinking it to be the best thing to do at that point when there is no time. We may be gaining time, but at what cost? Time is in our mind and only if we understand that virtual emotions are extremely harmful and would take one to the level of loneliness, emotional disconnect and depression, then we would surely earmark time in the routine to be with our near and dear ones.

In a virtual emotional connect, it is said that one generally projects only the positives, the gains, and sometimes, situations and events which are not actually true. There is hardly any confidence built or a clear understanding or consoling support which only real-time emotional connect can give. Nobody is able to open up and share problems truly. All interactions are superficial. Today, with advancements in technology, we fail to realize that the gains and this prosperity are not the true need of humans, but, real-time emotional and social connect that we all crave for.

We find there is a big gap between what we express in virtual connect and what we really mean. Even to the extent that in reality, we are separated emotionally from our family, our children, our parents, our relatives, friends and colleagues. Many a time, the husband and wife live in different places due to job requirements and connect with each other only virtually. How strong can the bonding be, especially if they have not even got to know each other very well? All are virtual transactions and the consequences would be similar to holding virtual currency not knowing the real value and where it will lead to.

Not only is virtual emotional connection harmful, which can lead to loneliness, it is essentially dangerous in fact. We have heard of a number of cases where young minds are lured through online emotional connect with criminals. They get trapped by the miscreants; all caused by falling prey virtually and going into high stress or depression or are forced to take extreme steps. They are made to believe the virtual emotions are true while actually they are not. Cyber crime is mostly rooted in virtual emotion. When the very identity of the person we are connecting with is not certain, how can the emotions we share ever be true? So many frauds take place in every field including on matrimonial sites, where we do not know if the details given are genuine or not.

One has to spend time in person to get emotionally connected. A tea, a get-together, a game or an open talk with your subordinates would go a long way to connect with them and help them open up to you. It would make you approachable, give that human touch to you, and make you feel good throughout your life.

Even after 40 years, my men who spent just two years with me are still in touch with me. I am still connected with all my soldiers—Bhoop Singh, Mota Ram, Bhanni Singh, Ravinder, Hanumana, Bhagwana—and can recollect everyone by their names and feel the emotional connect.

Today we have many virtual groups where we exchange wishes and news from all over the world and feel happy with all the false emotions. Mostly, we live in a make-believe world of 'forwards' and of wishing one another 'Good Morning' or 'Happy Birthday'. Do we really feel connected with them or are we living in a bubble? Can we do something about removing the virtual glasses we wear and replace them with real emotions?

Think it over.

✧✧✧✧✧

# CHAPTER 2

# MY COVID FILES

## 2.1 Get to the Basics

***Dhyan se Rehana aur Jo karna hai, Dil se Karna!***

(*Written during the beginning of the first wave of the pandemic*)

If you cannot go outside, then go inside!

When I say inside, it is not only staying indoors due to the lockdown because of the sudden entry made by an unknown microbe, which has put the whole world on pause mode, but also spending time to look inwards and searching within ourselves. Everything that is happening these days is unprecedented and unexpected. This is not the time to panic or get carried away in a wave of tension. There are many productive ways to spend the time which has suddenly become unending and everlasting.

We are being bombarded by so many thoughts, ideas, views, opinions, and outlooks from all sides. I'll touch upon three aspects which I think are key ways to tide over these difficult times. They are self-discipline, health, and faith.

## *Self-Discipline*

Implicit obedience to our conscience is the need of the hour. All of us know what has to be done, all the do's and don'ts and are aware of all the facts. In fact, we have been flooded with so much information that we want to keep our heads above all this and allow some sanity to sink in. The lockdown has been imposed, but these are no arbitrary orders. Let us understand the heart of the issue and follow it for our own safety. We stay inside, not only because we are following the Centre's orders but also because we know it is for our own good. Resolve and restraint are the key words. Resolve to stay indoors and restrain from breaking the orders. Self-discipline will ensure this. Let us be disciplined and maintain a high level of hygiene, ensure social distancing and spend quality time at home.

Self-discipline is not doing what our mind wants us to do but doing what is actually right to do. The answer is within us, in our subconscious mind. Let us use our brains, not our minds; think and respond, not react; use prudence and be conscious of all that we do. Social distancing is the answer to stay safe. Let us be with our family and quarantine ourselves from the rest of the world. It is difficult but possible! No travel, no visitors, and no helpers—be by ourselves alone. We have to learn to spend time by and with ourselves independently.

The economically better and the more advanced nations have fallen prey to this little bit of DNA enclosed in a layer of lipid only because of lack of self-discipline. No amount of external enforcement can achieve this if we are not ourselves convinced about it. No one else but I am in charge of my good health and if being disciplined will ensure it, then, why not go ahead with it?

### *Good Health*

Staying in good health is our responsibility. The need of the hour is to build up immunity. We have to ensure that our body is well tuned and ready to fight the disease if it affects us. There are stories where people have survived even the gas chambers in concentration camps during World War II. Then, there are people who have been in solitary confinement for years together and have come out of it in a good state of physical and mental health—all because they maintained a focused purpose to win and exercised to keep body and mind in good form. If they could do it, so can we. Foolhardiness or street smartness will not fight the disease; it is purely the in-built resistance to fight the microbe and the immunity developed in us that will overpower the tiny organism. Exercise, Yoga, Pranayam, walking or aerobics and activities like dancing and gardening are all good for building stamina and staying robust.

He who has health has hope and he who has hope has everything. As our Honourable Prime Minister said in his speech announcing the 21-day lockdown, *"Jaan hai to Jahan hai"* meaning if there is life, then the world is ours to conquer. It is in our hands to ensure we stay in good health and do not fall prey to this tiny microbe. We must stay in good health not only to beat the organism but also for our own well-being.

If we can motivate our family to do yoga as a group, it will act as a force multiplier. These exercises along with breathing exercises will boost energy levels and ensure we are in top form with a high level of immunity against any disease.

For a healthy body, if exercise is the answer, for a sound, strong and alert mind, doing regular prayers is a source of strength and solace. More things are wrought through prayer than this world dreams of. Other ways of engaging the mind and staying mentally robust are reading good books, listening to pleasant and elevating music, doing mind games and solving puzzles. Keeping ourselves fruitfully occupied inside the house—learning to cook, taking care of indoor plants, doing deep cleaning, playing indoor games, completing all the pending backlog of work, consolidating accounts, organizing funds, planning for the future, spending time to catch up with friends and relatives we've not had time to talk to, planning and learning anything new are some of the ways to spend time productively and effectively and also ways to keep the mind active and agile.

### *Faith*

Positive thinking is the key to faith. The mind is the strongest source and as our thoughts, so our life. SO, LET US CULTIVATE POSITIVE, ENRICHING, REJUVENATING THOUGHTS TO STAY HEALTHY AND STRONG. Faith can even move mountains. As mentioned under health, prayer is the answer to all problems. God may not always answer but we want, but HE always answers the prayers we need. "Therefore I tell you whatever you ask for in prayer believe that you have received it, and it will be yours."—Mark 11:24. All religions advocate the same point that with Faith everything can be accomplished. Faith in prayers and God is one thing; the other is faith in oneself. So, that is where a positive mind reinforcing positive thoughts plays a role.

In times of crisis, if we have the tenacity, we can come out stronger and evolve into tougher and better-equipped people. It is said necessity is the mother of invention. I am sure we will find ways to conquer the crisis and make it an opportunity for expanding our horizons. In these trying and desperate times, they would say desperate measures would be required, but I feel simplicity holds the key—like it is said—back to basics—concentrate and focus on the basics—

self-discipline, good health and faith that we will tide over these difficult days. This too shall pass and we will once again have bright, happy, healthy times soon. Now is the chance to show the world that we are a young, vigilant, and united country and that we can fight what might seem so insurmountable. Together, we can create history.

*(I would like to appreciate all volunteers who have been unmindful of their personal comfort and have come forward to provide all essential support and take care of the needy and keep them going during the lockdown. A salute to you.)*

✧✧✧✧✧

## 2.2 Being in the Present

### Now and Here

*(This article was written during the first COVID-19 lockdown)*

In this article I would like to address an important issue—INTERNALIZATION—or, we can say, introspection or seeing within ourselves. (This subject is of value at all times, but was ideal when all of us were locked down in our homes and shut out from our day-to-day routine.)

At such a time, (in fact, most of the time), our mind is making too much noise. It is said that 80 to 90 per cent of most people's thinking is not only repetitive and useless but also dysfunctional and often negative in nature, and, mostly harmful. Just observe your mind and you will find this to be true. It causes a serious drain of vital energy. This is actually an addiction. You no longer feel that you have the choice to stop. It also gives a sense of "pleasure", pleasure that invariably turns into pain.

The work of the mind is to operate the thoughts. Mostly they are the outcome of our experiences and future expectations. These thoughts, though not true, still make us believe them as real. Based on these, emotions in the form of fear, threat, anger, and happiness emerge. All these are destructive. Eckhart Tolle urges, "Do not identify yourself with your mind." The mind that operates based on the past or the future adds no value but only gives pain. Therefore, when we look at our mind, we should look at it as an observer, as a third person. Then we will realize that most thoughts die by themselves, if we do not identify with them.

The process of being an observer/watcher of one's mind without identifying with our thoughts is not easy. In fact, the mind is a machine that has to analyse thoughts. Thinking is always good but, thinking of the past or the likely future will only cause disturbance. Then what should we do? Think of the present, that is, the HERE and NOW.

We and our minds are not one. They are separate and we should never identify ourselves with our minds. We should act NOW, do what has to be done in the present and not get influenced by the mind which imagines what might or might not happen in the future. In fact, if the mind is left to work, it will create an obsession with the future. The future is a replica of the past! The past is what was "NOW" at that time. So, what we perceive as the future is actually an intrinsic part of our state of consciousness now, the present. So we have to train our minds to see the now and when it drifts to the past or the future, we must stop identifying with it. If we treat those irrelevant thoughts like uninvited guests in our home, our minds will automatically start working on Now. Finally, to live in the present alone will give us joy.

Everyone wants to be joyous and happy but happiness is not the same as pleasure. There is a lot of difference between pleasure and joy. Joy comes from within while pleasure is derived from outside, that is, out of ego-gratification and from things we identify with, in order to fill the hole we feel within. These are striving after possessions, money, success, power, and recognition that we perceive we get from the work we do, social status, knowledge, education, physical appearance, special ability, relationships, personal and family history. Basically, we want it because we can feel better about ourselves, feel more complete. However, even after we attain all these things, we still feel that the hole is still there. It is bottomless. As long as our mind is running our life, we cannot truly be at ease. Also, since pleasure is derived out of ego, and is identified with external things, it has to be defended and fed constantly. However, none of these is us. When we get them, we think we are happy but, actually, it is only pleasure. Remember, that external things are never permanent. So when they leave or end, we are sad and experience pain. So, our minds are always in turmoil.

What we must seek instead, is joy. It is within us. It is always bliss. If we have it then we are full of joy and if not, we are just without it. We do not experience pain. How do we get it? It is by disassociating ourselves from our mind and, not identifying with it. In fact, we have to be a master over our mind and not a part of it because the mind has a tendency to justify the past or future leaving us with only desires, wants, and fears.

Remember, our mind is not us. We have to focus on NOW and train our minds to think and focus on now. Let us be in the present and watch our minds, our thoughts and emotions as well as our reactions in various situations. We should not judge or analyze what we observe and not make the thoughts in our minds our personal problem to resolve. As we watch with intense presence and set the goal and work for this moment, we are full of joy.

Let lockdowns not create turbulence in our minds about the uncertain future. Let us train our minds to work for the Present—the Now. Thoughts that emerge in our minds about our past or unrevealed future are not real. They are impediments to our present and drain our energy. The lockdown is like a tunnel. When we pass through an unknown tunnel, although we do not know for how long, light is sure to come. So, let us not keep wasting energy and brooding on imaginary thoughts but keep going on with the present. Focus on NOW and 'Being in the present' and find true happiness.

> *"Between stimulus and response there is a space. In that space is our power to choose our response. In our response lies our growth and freedom."*
>
> —**Viktor Frankl,** a well known psychiatrist and concentration camp survivor

✧✧✧✧✧

## 2.3 Ambiguity

### A Period of Uncertainty

(*Written during the first COVID wave*)

When everything we have seen, heard or read does not have any semblance of connection with what is happening in the present, we feel that our life and work has turned upside-down, chaotic, disorganized, and disarranged. The world seems to have turned topsy-turvy in our lifetime. An experience we never had before. We hear lots of news, ifs and buts, wild guesses and opinions freely floating around about things in store for us. We are now in a period of ambiguity and we have very little information about the novel corona virus, its effects, and how the future is going to be from here. Nothing seems certain or clear, there are so many questions but no answers.

How long will this uncertainty last? Will it ever come to an end? What should I do? Will things return to normal? Will I recover my business or job? Should I remain invested or pull out my shares? Will I maintain good health and do I have enough resources to handle it? What about my children's education? How about my mother's wellbeing? I am in the hospitality sector, should I change my job? My son is in the USA, will he retain his job? The list of questions is infinite but the answers are nebulous.

In spite of all the uncertainty it does not mean that life or work will stop. We have to be far-sighted enough to prevail over them and handle each situation as it is revealed. There is a beautiful quotation which states, "Don't be in such a rush to figure everything out. Embrace the unknown and let your life surprise you." This is a time to develop that part of the brain which can quickly analyze and take correct decisions with minimum data. Work through ambiguity. It is also time to be open to accept all changes.

Soldiers are trained to operate in situations of ambiguity. Decisions have to be made on the spot, often without adequate information. Only flexibility in thinking and adaptability would enable them to successfully accomplish their mission. In war, as ever so often in life too, decisions cannot be taken with 100 per cent information and predictability. With insufficient information, the leader has to take the plunge, believing in himself and his team and be prepared to shoulder the responsibility that comes with that decision. Again, in life, as in war, it is always better to take a decision than not take one. Fortune always favours the brave.

As a soldier, I remember that I was once tasked with my unit to capture an enemy post on the ridge line. My superiors at our Formation HQ were confident that the area was not occupied and would be easy to take over. However, when we started our reconnaissance, to our surprise, we found the ridge to be strongly held by a platoon plus of the enemy, who effectively dominated all possible approaches by observation and fire, making any attempt to assault the feature a costly proposition in terms of possible casualties. We were also not aware as to what was in store for us beyond the ridge line. Did the enemy have additional troops and support weapons on the top of the feature, or on the reverse slopes? Having received our orders to attack and capture the feature, we had no choice, but to go ahead with our mission with all odds against us and the probability of success being almost nil. It was a period of high uncertainty and extreme risk. Unless one takes the first step we reach nowhere. As soldiers, we are prepared for such eventualities, having trained for them and we know that we have to move ahead, come what may, regardless of the consequences.

Our troops were spread out as we had to climb along the steep spurs of the mountain slopes. Our movement had to be executed right under the nose of the enemy and we had no place to hide or take cover. When the operation commenced, with us climbing the steep rocky slopes in broad daylight, we were very fortunate when the entire area became blanketed with dense fog. Miraculously, the fog appeared to move along with us, for six hours, thereby preventing the enemy from observing our movements! However, they did open fire blindly with small arms and their artillery. We could see and hear the sound of splinters, shells, and shrapnel flying all around us. However, by the grace of God, none of us sustained any injury. The group which was sent through the toughest route managed to reach the summit and entrench themselves at a vantage point dominating the enemy. The enemy panicked and resorted to wild firing. Our troops, who had a better view now, became enterprising and more energized to take them on. The battle lasted for two days and our troops finally captured the three posts and turned a NO GO situation into a NOW GROW success situation. Such situations are very common for soldiers who are operating in situations of disadvantage and total ambiguity. They manage to turn the tables completely in their favour.

We have been used to a predictable life so far, planning and executing what has to be done but, this situation has turned everything inside out, compelling us to look at life from a different perspective. It has definitely given us an opportunity and time to introspect and really value so many things we simply took for granted so far.

Like our Honourable Prime Minister said, let us learn to look at the present COVID-19 situation as an opportunity instead of as a threat. This is the time to work to become self reliant and to focus on our internal strengths, our own personal as well as our nation's demography (the study of India's population, its size, growth, density and distribution), human resources, innovation and technology and encouraging local and national or Swadeshi instead of multinational and foreign.

In these testing times, no one knows when life will get back to "normal" as we knew it, whether it will at all, or, the present way of life with masks and social distancing and super hygiene will become the new normal. One can expect a second and third wave of attack. One way to view the present crisis is to be depressed looking at the looming threat to life and livelihood and say, "What can I do?" Another way to look at this COVID situation is to be passive and accept our predicament and wait it out, because it will have to end sooner or later. The proactive way to face it would be to ask not what, but "HOW can I do things to improve our situation?" We have to learn to take decisions in a correct frame of mind and learn to look at life in a new way. When the effects and results are unpredictable, we realize the options and opportunities are multifarious. This is an opportunity to discover new alternatives instead of treading the beaten path. A successful person is one who is ready to work when the outcome is predictable, but an outstanding person is one who is ready even when the result is unknown, indefinite, and unpredictable. If things have to move as predicted then where is innovation? Risk mitigation? Redrawing our journey? Understanding the self? Testing our belief and faith?

Let us learn to make life simple, lie low when the tide is high, revisit our basics according to our traditional style of living, understand our strengths, and work on being self reliant. Let us hold strongly to an anchor—Faith—to give us strength when doubts and fears rush in. Keeping our spiritual life form in a high state and maintaining a healthy routine will be a great source of energy. Let us tell ourselves that all of us (old and young, experienced and inexperienced) are all on the same platform for finding solutions in this period of ambiguity. It is only the brave, mentally strong and those ready to explore opportunities during times of crises that get the reward. Swami Vivekananda has said, "Know that the mind which is born to succeed joins itself to a determined will and perseveres."

Sticking to a well planned routine in our daily lives will give a sense of confidence and stability. As the situation unfolds, let us also be prepared to be flexible and adaptable to the change according to the need of the hour, be prepared for a new environment—social, economical and cultural transformations. Let us work with all possibilities to discover the best option to take life from here to a higher level.

In the history of mankind, it is during situations of great uncertainty, confusion, fear and ambiguity that something new and better has evolved. In this case also, the same is certain to happen. To paraphrase the words of the famous poet, Alfred Tennyson, "The old order (will) change, yielding place to the new."

✧✧✧✧✧

## 2.4 Purity

### Aacharam—A Leaf Out of Our Past

(*Written sometime before the second wave overtook us*)

Our life has come round a full circle!

Just about a year ago we found it amusing that people of the older generation maintained a 'decent' distance with others to avoid being touched, ate only home-cooked food, wore only freshly washed clothes and generally stayed away from gatherings and said it was because they had to pray! And now, fast forward to the present....A new term 'Social Distancing' has been coined to express the new way of living (actually an oxymoron, for, how can you be social and maintain distance at the same time!), and a NEW NORMAL has come into being. It is all thanks to the tiny COVID-19 virus! The mask and the sanitizer have become part of our dress code, now, we too maintain distance with people, avoid crowds and as soon as we come home from our place of work or shopping we sanitize ourselves.

We had managed to come out of a long period of lockdown after the first wave of corona but may be heading towards another one again as the second wave seems to be taking over probably because we have already forgotten all that we had learnt during the first wave.

India had been seen as an exemplar of the perfect model to follow as the world wondered how with such a huge population, we were able to contain the spread of the infection and flatten the curve better than other countries. The age-old Indian custom of greeting each other with a *namaste* (I bow to the God within you) had taken the world by storm and has more supporters than the typical smart Western handshake or the definitely more affectionate hug. Let us also remember to follow it because, distancing has had a strong effect in reducing the spread of the infection.

Recently, a talk by a scholar opened my eyes to a totally new dimension of the Indian way of life. He spoke of AACHARAM from Hindu Sanatana Dharma. I had heard the term earlier but had always associated it with the practices followed by saints and sadhus. I was stunned when he used the very word for ordinary people like us and also asked us to follow it in our day-to-day-life! He said it is meant for all, not only for sanyasis. According to him, there is no single equivalent word in English which can convey the meaning, but it can be explained by two words—CONDUCT and CHARACTER. Aacharam works at two levels: one External, good CONDUCT, and two, Internal, good CHARACTER. It involves maintaining external as well as internal PURITY. This purity is not limited to external cleanliness alone, (We know that cleanliness is next to godliness) but, also implies purity both in thought and action.

In fact, Aacharam refers to a way of life—a Hindu way of life or the path prescribed by the Sanatana Dharma. It is similar to the "New Normal" which has been forced upon us by nature now, and the earlier we learn to get used to it, the better for us. Everyone must respect Nature, follow social norms and the prescribed cultural restraint, and have a sense of responsibility in conduct and behaviour, that is, we must have SELF-DISCIPLINE. This is possible only when the driving force is from within. Without good character, mere good conduct, the external projection, would be like a beautiful building without a strong foundation. The new normal has to be accepted from within, the need for purity and cleanliness has to be self realized.

This new way of life is not for my safety alone but for the safety of the entire community. For the safety of our near and dear ones, let us follow the SOPs (Standard Operating Procedures) and protocols and remember that discipline must come not from outside; rather, it should come from within. It must not be something which is enforced but which comes automatically through realization. If we have to wear a mask, there is no point having it on our jaw like a coloured beard. If we wear it only when we will be punished or fined for not wearing it, then the act is just ornamental, not yet fundamental. After more than a year since the pandemic struck the world and even after the vaccines have started being administered, the mask continues to be one of the best ways of protection, along with of course staying in well-ventilated and open places, avoiding crowds, maintaining distance and ensuring proper hygiene. In the case of COVID-19, since it spreads exponentially and quickly, we are putting the entire society at danger if we flout rules—of not only contracting the disease but also of contracting a disease which might prove to be fatal. So, what all this finally boils down to is going back to our roots of "Vasudhaiva Kutumbakam", meaning 'the world is one family' which elucidates our country's global outlook.

Let us not limit ourselves to wearing masks, sanitizing our hands and the work space and maintaining social distance with the fear of getting ticked off but let the realization come from within and as a social responsibility. That is where Aacharam plays a role. It is our responsibility to take care of our health not only for ourselves but also for those around us. That is the meaning of the inner and outer element. Our inner power makes us do what is right, not for show but because we understand, care and know. To maintain good health from inside we have to ensure we have the correct diet, follow a good routine, exercise, and improve our immunity. A step further to this is to have purity of mind, develop positive energy, and lead a simple life. A person's character should shine through his actions and conduct. In fact, it is said that people who are considered superior are considered so because of the superiority in their character and behaviour.

So, let us reflect on this wonderful inspiring thought and practice Aacharam in our life—good conduct with good character (externally appropriate behaviour combined with internally being socially responsible). These corona times have been instrumental in bringing back our forgotten customs to the fore and reminding us of our core values. Let us imbibe them and be role models for the world. As such, the world is looking towards India for more reasons than one—let this be the primary one.

We will surely return to our old secure way of life but we must carry forward into our new lives the wisdom and teachings which this unique situation has thrown upon us.

✧✧✧✧✧

## 2.5 Prudence is a 'Must'

### An Experience with COVID

(*Written during the second wave of Corona*)

"You can never understand the problem unless you have experienced it", my friend told me. He had just come out of the hospital after a difficult stay in the ICU and having had a devastating experience during the second wave of COVID-19 in 2021.

I offered some words of comfort.

My friend said, "Even my worst enemy should not experience it." He was referring to the current corona situation. "There is nothing like 'the virus is gone." If you slacken your guard, in all probability, you will fall a victim to it. Not worth it. Better to pull up our socks and learn to live with the correct protocol. If you visit a doctor, it is his moment to fill his purse by charging you Rs 1,500 per visit for consultancy. If you are lucky, you may get the appointment in hours. The difficulty in getting admission and oxygen support is only one part of the story; even the person who comes to give the oxygen will come only if you grease his palm well."

I said, "I agree. Very sad. We have lost many lives. Probably, the same could have been avoided with good discipline and health care."

"You are right, it was a matter of one wrong exposure of mine, which not only made a hole in my purse costing me Rs. 3,00,000 but was also an experience of loneliness; in fact, a feeling of being deserted by everyone during the isolation period in the hospital which was the worst punishment meted out to me in my life. Even my spouse and my dear ones were helpless and were not allowed to meet me and I had no energy to spend time on my mobile either. What we crave for and bitterly miss is the presence of another human being who loves you, by your side. The whole episode seemed so impersonal. I saw death at very close quarters. I prayed to God that I may please be given a chance to be able to inform people that this experience is not worth it. Many were not so fortunate to come out alive despite spending a fortune."

"Umm, you had an indescribable experience. Am I right?"

"Yes, No words can really get close to the actual. Your apprehension starts right from the time you are alone waiting in the queue to be allotted a bed in the hospital. In addition, my intake went down...I was unable to eat anything. My throat pained and I had terrible bouts of coughing. I had fever and the fatigue was immense. In spite of the fact that my oxygen level was ok, it was a miserable experience."

"Oh, that's bad. But, thank God for small mercies. At least your oxygen level was good."

"True, but you were always worried about what could happen the next moment. Most of the treatment was based on my clinical conditions and my discharge looked remote. I was not worried about death, but the incident made me realize the value of life that we take for granted."

"Now that you are perfectly fine, I am sure you will ensure double safety. Once bitten twice shy?"

"That's correct."

Through my friend, I understood the severity of the situation. It reinforced what I already knew. Coming from someone who had just scraped through, it was an eye opener that we must not let our guard down at any point. Not even after vaccination. People become over-confident and think that it will protect them from contracting corona. The vaccination is like wearing a seat belt in a car. If you wear it, it does not protect you from accidents but definitely prevents it from becoming fatal. The same is the case with vaccination. Even if you get the disease, you will definitely recover. To be safe, is to drive your life securely by following safety instructions and taking all precautions.

To add to this is what the Ugandan president said in a speech, "God has lot of work; he has the whole world to look after. He cannot be just here in Uganda looking after idiots...It is a war without mercy. It is without any milk of human kindness. It is indiscriminate....it is an invisible, fleet footed and ruthlessly effective army...thankfully, this army has a weakness and it can be defeated. It only requires collective action, discipline, and forbearance. COVID cannot survive social and physical distancing. It thrives when you confront it...but it bows before good physical hygiene...." We agree. The same applies to India also. By sheer flouting of social distancing norms in the recent past, we have allowed cases to surge uncontrollably. The second wave has hit India like a tornado.... We had become complacent when we found we were better off than the other nations when the first wave swept through the world. COVID spreads due to human negligence and carelessness. With every mistake we make, we are helping the virus to spread exponentially but, if we follow the right protocol, it has to perish.

If we learn to go with Nature it will never go out of its way to harm us but if we challenge it, Natural Law will take its course. If today's environment calls for a certain protocol, we should follow it. We can deceive a human but not nature. For getting into trouble, age and physical condition is no bar. Nature is ruthless. It does not differentiate between young or old, weak or strong. Good health may protect you from the worst but even that is not assured. Let us all understand the situation and follow norms without being told or checked. Let us remember to be responsible. This is an epidemic. It requires collective action. Just one lapse is sufficient to start the next wave. Let us all work to stop the occurrence of a third wave. Let us look at this experience as something that has taught us a lot about life and not forget to always be disciplined, never let our guard down and remember these lessons even when everything is back to normal, as, remembering the lessons from the past will ensure we do not commit any mistake again.

Mankind will remember THIS WAR—

*A war that was fought by DOCTORS, not soldiers*
*A war that was fought with SOAP, not guns*
*A war that was fought by Keeping DISTANCE, not contact*
*A war that was fought from HOME, not on the battlefield*

*A good soldier fights with PRUDENCE*

✧✧✧✧✧

## 2.6 My Thoughts

### *The Virus in the Mind is More dangerous than the Virus Outside*

(*Written during the third wave when Omicron put the world on hold*)

Change is inevitable, that is the law of life but, how we become part of the change or cause the change to happen or how we handle the change which takes place, whether we are passive bystanders or are ourselves actively involved in the change going on, whether it is a positive or a negative one, a change for the better or worse, whether the change will usher in something desirable or will it be distasteful will have to be seen.

Take the COVID-19 virus for example. It took the world by storm and how the world has seen a sea change after 2020 is clear for all to see. The virus has not remained static, either. It has also evolved over the last two years and so many variants and mutants have come up. However, humankind too has not been twiddling its thumbs. Scientists and researchers have been working round the clock to find a solution. Of the so many new variants that have surfaced, some have been labelled as variants of concern and some as variants of interest, depending on whether we have to protect ourselves from them or learn something new! The speed at which a variety of vaccines have been produced, tested, and given to individuals the world over, is simply astounding! It shows the immense capability of man. If this is the accomplishment shown by the scientific fraternity, on the other front, the common people have not lagged behind too—so many people have adapted themselves to the new way of life, and not only survived but also found new opportunities created by the new world post corona.

We have all heard that there are good and bad bacteria whereas viruses are only harmful and can only cause damage to the human body and life in general. However, actually there are some manipulated virus species which are helpful to cure human genetic disorders and cancer and are used in RDNA technology. Mostly they have DNA as genetic material, not RNA. "Virotherapy"—this term is used when with the help of viruses we are able to cure a disorder or disease. So, everything is double-edged, it depends on the user. Humans have used the corona virus itself for treating COVID-19, making vaccines in different ways—weakening the virus, deactivating it, using part of the virus, using mRNA from it and so on!

Now, there is a new strain of virus or mutant of corona, "Omicron", which has come into existence, first reported to the World Health Organization (WHO) from South Africa on 24 November 2021. It is a variant of SARS-CoV-2, the virus that causes COVID-19. On 26 November 2021, the WHO designated it as a variant of concern and named it 'Omicron', after the fifteenth letter in the Greek alphabet. Scientists are working on a fast track to find a way to overcome this new virus variant.

The term 'virus' actually originates from a Greek word which means poison. Is poison always harmful? There is historical evidence to show that the great king, Chandragupta Maurya, was being given minute doses of poison in his food by his minister, Acharya Chanakya. He was doing this to actually increase the king's immunity against poison because in those days the emperor was susceptible to various threats by enemies, especially in the form of poison. As the king had been consuming poison in very small quantities for long, his body had developed resistance against larger doses of poison and had become stronger. So, we can see that poison itself has two sides, positive and negative. Similarly, though viruses are harmful for our body, if the right course of action is followed, we can prevail over them too.

Following natural law, the corona virus and all other viruses will keep taking new forms as mutation is an ongoing and normal process, but human beings, as a race, have something that is capable of withstanding the onslaught of all the different variants and mutants which keep cropping up from time to time—that is the power of the mind!

> *"The mind is its own place, and in itself, can make a Heaven of Hell, a Hell of Heaven."*
>
> —**John Milton**

Our mind could be the real cause for the virus or it could become an antidote for it! It can be a catalyst to make the case worse if we let it float without control. A common phenomenon called 'addiction and power of random reinforcement' happens when we listen to the news looking for minute to minute updates. What we do not realize is that unknown to us, this increases fear, anxiety, apprehension, stress, and unease within us which lowers our immunity. Though awareness is necessary, there should not be a morbid addiction to news. We keep listening hoping for some word of assurance amidst all the negative deluge. So, in the anticipation of hearing something reassuring we are meanwhile reinforcing negative facts in our mind. To be certain that we are not missing out on some important information which will make us feel safer and more secure, we are obsessed and keep watching or reading the news. This actually has a damaging effect on us and keeps us anxious, worried and uneasy which affects the nervous system because we are continuously looking for rewards (immediate news on the virus) and get addicted to the updated data and numbers. Our mind keeps on analyzing, updating, and justifying (the reason to see the news), which fills it with fretful thoughts faster than the virus-spread itself.

During stressful conditions the level of stress hormones like Cortisol increases in the body which has a detrimental effect on the mind and body. Anxiety and stress take us to levels which make us think irrationally too. For those who hesitated to get themselves vaccinated, their minds would have justified why taking vaccinations was dangerous and harmful to health. They would have gathered data to prove why it should be avoided. Even when its safety had been proved beyond doubt, their minds would have refused to accept it. This poison in the mind is more harmful than the virus itself.

On the other hand, our minds can be an antidote or a way to conquer the virus if we can think in the right direction—this can actually change things. Scientists and others working to find new ways to overcome the virus use that faculty of the mind to find new solutions for mankind. Even a layman can outsmart the virus if he uses his mind to follow the right methods to build up immunity. Our immunity, if developed, is capable of overthrowing the akaryote (i.e., a cell without a nucleus). Along with building our immunity, we can also strengthen another aspect within us—our mind power (will power)

The mind power of humans can do anything. Mind power is not just a term; it is the characteristic trait of human beings. By using it, the human brain can increase the metabolic rate which boosts energy generation which ultimately enhances the efficiency of the immune system. It always becomes visible when a person goes through very hard times and in cases of physical pain too—is he able to surmount the problem or not? It depends a lot on his mind- the power of the mind is stronger than anything that can affect us. It is greater than any other power in the world and also any medicine. There are many cases of hopeless medical conditions which could be conquered by the will of the individual. But mind power is not inherited—this implies that it can be imbibed or learnt by anyone who wishes to—by anyone who uses his own free will. Such a person will be able to do anything in his life.

In many of the cases during the second wave of COVID-19, the rise in the panic level due to the fear factor made the situation critical. The pessimistic and defeatist attitude reduced the chances of recovery further, whereas those with strong minds and a positive outlook who had confidence that "this too shall pass" were able to battle all the demons and come out fighting fit. They were able to return home safe and sound. Keeping the mind calm during stressful situations and affirming the right things to ourselves is the way forward. By using our mind power, we can increase the level of hormones like Serotonin and Dopamine, both of which are responsible for the happiness of a person. If our mind power is strong, it will increase our metabolism and also energy production and with that the level of these two hormones will also increase which will create an auto therapy for our ourselves. So, the mind plays a great role and it is for us to feed it with positive, reassuring information instead of negative and disquieting ones.

To prove that our words and thoughts have an effect on our very being and influence it powerfully, a scientist experimented on water to check the effect of different sounds on it. He took water in 40 tubes and placed them in different sound mediums having different energy levels. He placed the first one where there was sacred chanting, the second near a rock band orchestra, the third where a person was depressed and spoke negatively, the fourth one where the speaker was giving a motivational speech emphasizing the positive outlook, the fifth where children were playing and where there were sounds of laughter and so on. After that, he collected all the samples and froze them at minus 4 degrees

Celsius temperature and observed the crystal formation in the snow flakes. He was stunned to see the results.

There was a marked difference between the structures formed in happy, positive frequency places as compared with places with sad, negative, or angry moods. When placed in positive, loving conditions, the crystalline structure was even, ordered and beautiful whereas in unhappy or negative situations, the formation was disorganised and distorted. Our body is mostly made up of water, so it is obvious how much our words and thoughts will affect us from within. Every cell of the body can be made to orient itself in a particular direction, based on what kind of thoughts and words we feed it with. This is because of our mind which has the power to control our thoughts and actions.

We have the free will to choose what kind of thoughts we want to fill our mind with. If we think positive, happy thoughts, our immunity will increase which will ultimately kill all negative particles including viruses. The virus which affects us will not be the one from outside, entering our body, but the virus from within which has entered the mind. The virus in the mind is more dangerous than the actual virus itself and it cannot enter unless we allow it to. If the water in the test tubes can be influenced so much to show such vast variations in the snowflake formation, think of how much more the water in each cell of our body will respond to optimistic, productive, cheerful, creative and buoyant thoughts. So let us always be hopeful and have faith in the greater design of things. This will ensure our immunity levels are high and no virus can enter the circle of protection which we have made around ourselves.

✧✧✧✧✧

# CHAPTER 3

# LEARNING AND DEVELOPMENT

## 3.1 Beyond Classroom Learning

### *Open Learning vs. Closed Learning*

What do we do after our schooling? Look for a college? Start from the top ten colleges listed on online sites? Look for where to give entrance exams? Choose a well-known institution, pick up a branch that is sought for by all, and finally get into an administratively viable one? It is simple. The purpose is to quickly get the best package job after passing out from college. However, do we really know that there is a lot more than getting an entry into a company?

A classroom always equips us with knowledge but success is not measured by knowledge alone. In olden days, when we had the gurukul type of education which was open, and focused on holistic development, the guru dedicatedly monitored the capability of the students—their ability to absorb knowledge, their aptitude and ability to practically apply their mind and body to the learnt skills.

From the same guru, Arjun became a bowman/archer; Duryodhan became an expert in *gada yudh*; Bhim in *malyudh*; Sahadeva in rearing cows; Nakul in horses and animals. Surely they would have been misfits if their roles had been reversed. While they were given all-round holistic training, their specialization was in their individual taste and personal inclination. It was never restricted to classroom learning alone and 'one size fits all' kind of learning.

How does this translate in the modern system? We must have the knowledge and adequate exposure to explore beyond classroom lessons. The three 'H's that we call...Head, Heart and Hands must be involved. The head is necessary for acquiring knowledge but, it is the heart, that is, attitude that makes things happen. Without involvement of the heart, there is no life, no taste, no enthusiasm, no entrepreneurship, or creativity. Passion is the key. Similarly, education is incomplete without acquiring hands-on exposure, experience, and skill. How many of us are really able to put the knowledge to actual use?

In the movie "3 Idiots", this aspect of Open Learning... learning beyond books, has been skilfully highlighted. The movie not only comes up as a criticism against the formatted mindset of society, but also encourages the students, their parents, and those in the field of education to be open to new ways of learning and to new fields of knowledge. It advocates going for what one's heart desires and pursuing it up to the finis instead of following the herd.

Learning and Development Programme in universities is there for the students to approach and develop skills that are essential for success. It could be just improving communication, introspection, discovering self or for developing such emotional intelligence as to be ready when launched into society after institutional training.

Let us answer this for ourselves. How much do we use

our labs? Do we know that we have innovative labs like idea labs and prototype labs in universities? Do we explore them? How many of us are using our finishing schools? Do we take time to participate in sports, social and cultural learning platforms? In the last one year, can we recollect one special aspect that we have developed or one skill that we have achieved or one game/sport/music that we have tried out? Did we put in that extra effort to improve our verbal communication/written ability or any such activity to develop confidence and personality?

Don't you think that classroom culture alone is not sufficient? Can we move out from this closed learning towards the boundless open learning as is advocated in the Rig Vedas—Let noble thoughts come to us from all directions—where we seek the knowledge that we desire, experiment hands-on and close in on that which we love the most?

Think it over.

✧✧✧✧✧

## 3.2 Communication

### Communication is an Art

All creatures communicate. The way a bee dances and flaps its wings, communicates to its hive where pollen can be found and how far it is. Similarly, bats determine through ultrasonic frequencies the dimensions of their surroundings and emit high-pitched sounds to communicate them. We are familiar with the way man's best friend, dogs, communicate using their wagging tails to express their delight and uncontrolled happiness on seeing their master. Their whining, growling and barking also are their ways of communicating. A cow moos and licks her calf to express her happiness, monkeys chatter and peacocks spread their wings and dance when the rain clouds build up. The whole world revolves around staying in touch and being connected with each other.

Humans have evolved from cave paintings to a very high level of communication in the present age so much so that the whole world is a mere global village. One gets to know whatever is happening in any part of the world within no time. It is believed the three fastest means of communication are: Tweeting, Telephoning and Telling a woman!

So what is Communication and why is it so important in the present day? Communication is about trying to recreate in the mind of the receiver what is in our mind. It is a two-way process in which there is a give-and-take of ideas, feelings, or thoughts, which is accepted by both sides or progresses towards it. In communication, words are important, but, words are not everything. The most important thing is hearing what is not said and figuring out what was actually conveyed. Understanding what is meant to be communicated is the goal of communication. A message is considered successful only when both sides perceive it in the same way.

However, as George Bernard Shaw rightly said, "The single biggest problem with communication is the illusion that it has taken place."—A new student from a non-English speaking background made everyone roar with laughter when she said, "I am like a banana", when asked by the teacher what fruit she liked! Another instance shows that miscommunication blunders can take place even in international markets. In the 1990s, there was one involving brand names and slogans. In Taiwan, Pepsi's slogan "Come Alive with the Pepsi Generation" when literally translated meant, "Pepsi will bring your Ancestors back from the Dead."!!!! So, communication is determined not by how well we say things, but how well we are understood.

Communication is a very important element of our lives and it is important for building relationships and for having a good rapport with others. According to the classical theory of communication, intrapersonal, interpersonal, group, and cultural are the four distinct levels of communication, depending on the number and kind of people involved. Cross-cultural communication is a field where the manner in which people from different cultures try to communicate is studied. In an organization with people of different cultures, becoming aware of the differences in beliefs, communication strategies, and business customs is essential. Communication acts as a bridge between cultures and as a force behind cultural change.

The world has a multitude of people and each person has his own perception of everything around him. "To effectively communicate, we must realize that we are all different in the way we perceive the world and use this understanding as a guide to our communication with others", asserts Tony Robbins.

The various types of communication are, Spoken or Verbal Communication, Non Verbal Communication, Written Communication and Visualizations (Messages can be communicated even pictorially through graphs and other visual aids.) In human one-on-one direct communication, the three major elements are body language, voice tonality, and words. Unlike what we might imagine, the maximum impact is by our non-verbal communication which includes body language—postures, gestures, and eye contact. The next important factor is the tone of our voice and, the actual content or the words has only 7 per cent impact! That is how some people are able to sway crowds with their gesticulations and by dramatic speaking. The way we speak has a greater impact than what we say—a bond has to be built between the speaker and the audience.

*Great communication begins with connection*. Communication is the foundation of human relationships. However, it does not always need words. A look, a touch, a gesture is sufficient. When a mother hugs her child, she is able to communicate a whole gamut of emotions where words would fall short. Paul J. Meyer, a great businessman, believed, communication skills are a must and investing our time on learning and getting better at how to communicate will stand us in good stead. Good communication is the forte of a good leader. He is able to convey his message clearly, motivate the listeners and inspire them to take the right action. "Communication—the human connection—is the key to personal and career success." Can we pick up communication skills? Yes, definitely.

Some are good at communicating from the beginning but others need not despair! It is a skill that can be learnt like cooking or dancing by working on it. The biggest problem is that we do not listen to understand, we listen to reply. **Listening attentively** is an essential skill in effective communication. People with effective communication skills first understand **who** they are communicating with. Accordingly, they mould their matter to suit the audience. A good communicator follows the three C's of communication—he is **clear, concise and correct** in his speech. He also displays **confidence**. He knows when to speak up and when to keep quiet. He is specific and straightforward and does not beat around the bush to confuse the listener. Those good at communication skills are adept at recognizing **non-verbal cues** too. Is the audience listening attentively or are the listeners distracted or bored or worried or excited or agitated? To be able to understand the pulse of the audience, a good communicator **uses questions** to gauge how much they have comprehended and also encourages questions to remove any confusion. This is a good method since each aspect can be dealt with thoroughly and the interest, attention, and focus of the audience can be held better than through a lecture. An interactive session is always more rewarding as the communicator can get his message across in an enhanced way. These are some handy techniques to become skilful in communicating.

When we see people together, we automatically assume communication is taking place but, it is not always so. When two people are talking, instead of a dialogue taking place, where there is give-and-take, if there are just two monologues, there is no bond or connection developed between the two of them. Each is expressing his viewpoint without hearing or showing any interest in the other. There has to be a linking factor to be connected. Many debates on critical topics by members from different political parties on TV border on the ludicrous because of this. Sometimes, we see speakers on the podium haranguing the audience without realizing the latter are not participating in the process at all. Similarly, when we hear or read Shashi Tharoor's bombastic and confounding language, we realize it will not reach most of the audience unless he is in the midst of literary aficionados. The familiar nursery rhyme "Jack and Jill went up the hill...." in his words become "Two individuals proceeded towards the apex of a natural geologic protuberance, the purpose of their expedition being the procurement of a sample of fluid hydride of oxygen in a large receptacle,...."!!!

When we wish to convey something, for communication to be successful, we must understand and identify with our message, the audience we are sending it to and also, how the audience will perceive it. The ability to express an idea is as important as the idea itself. Communication takes place only when the other person understands the essence of our words in the way we meant it. Putting it pithily and in a tongue-in-cheek manner, we can say, for communication to be successful, it must be a KISS and also HOT! - meaning, one must Keep It Short and Simple and it must be Honest, Open and Two-way. Only when both sides are interested and work to understand each other without any ambiguity will there be effective communication.

Abraham Lincoln's famous Gettysburg address took only two minutes and had just 246 words, whereas, before Lincoln, the then well-known orator Edward Everett, spoke 13,687 words for two hours! It could not have held the attention of the audience for long. Lincoln's oft-quoted words on democracy that it is "of the people, by the people and for the people" is still remembered because of its simplicity and brevity. It reaches the heart directly. Rosemary O'Neil reminds us that we must "Be brief and to the point, always, every time."

We can all imbibe the art of good communication by remembering that mere speaking for the sake of speaking is not communication. When we speak to people, it is not for getting them to do what we want them to do but to fill them with great delight and also, to reach their heart. For good communication, we should shake hands with a firm grip, maintain positive eye contact, pace our words appropriately and speak clearly; our language should be correct and our manner considerate; we should smile, be friendly and ensure that the way we speak and our body language match, give examples from real life to show the audience how we can help them; listen attentively and ask questions which show our comprehension and interest and understand the other person's requirements—can we satisfy him? These simple guidelines will go a long way in building a good relationship with others.

✧✧✧✧✧

## 3.3 All About Memory

### Interesting Facts About Memory

> *"The human brain can remember events, skills, habits, and experiences. The sum of what is remembered is called a memory."*
>
> —**Frank Knoll**

Let me share some interesting facts about our brain and memory. The brain is an amazing three-pound organ. It controls and coordinates actions and reactions, allows us to think and feel, and enables us to have memories and feelings. Did you know that memory starts to work just 20 weeks after conception and the human brain starts to remember things from the womb? The story of Abhimanyu in the *Mahabharata* and of Bhakth Prahalad learning to chant Vishnu's name from Sage Narada even before he was born prove this fact.

Have you ever thought how short 'Short-Term Memory' actually is? STM, also known as primary or active memory lasts only 20 to 30 seconds. It is the capacity to store a small amount of information in the mind (about 7 items + or minus 2) for a short period of time. We can check this out ourselves with this DIY experiment. Look at the list of words given below for two minutes and then write them down without seeing.

| Nine | Swap | Cell | Ring | Lust |
|---|---|---|---|---|
| Plugs | Lamp | Apple | Table | Sway |
| Army | Bank | Fire | Hold | Worm |
| Clock | Horse | Colour | Baby | Sword |
| Desk | Grab | Find | Bird | Rock |

Despite having two minutes to memorize the words, it is surprisingly difficult to recall even a handful of words. This experiment demonstrates some of the limitations of short-term memory. However, memory rehearsal strategies, such as Chunking, can significantly increase memorization and recall.

| | | | | |
|---|---|---|---|---|
| Horse | Cat | Dog | Fish | Bird |
| Orange | Yellow | Blue | Green | Black |
| Table | Chair | Desk | Bookcase | Bed |
| Teacher | School | Student | Homework | Class |
| Apple | Banana | Kiwi | Grape | Mango |

The above items, on the other hand, can be easily grouped based on category, so we can remember far more of these words. Clustering can be a useful memorization strategy that can improve the retention and recall of information.

Did you know that our brains can actually store a countless amount of information-up to 2.5 petabites of data? That is the equivalent of three million hours of TV shows—or about the same storage as nearly 4,000 256-GB iPhones!

Would you wonder if I told you how significant sleep is to memory? In addition to aiding in memory, sleep also plays an essential role in learning new information. It helps in the retrieval and storage of long-term memories. Research indicates that when memory is first recorded in the brain–in the hippocampus–it is still "fragile" and easily forgotten. Napping pushes the memories to the neocortex, the brain's "more permanent storage", preventing them from being "overwritten." While NREM sleep is important for restoring physiological functions, REM sleep is essential in restoring mental functions. During Slow Wave Sleep (SWS), declarative memory—memorization of facts—is encoded. In contrast, Rapid Eye Movement (REM) sleep is associated with the consolidation of procedural memory that involves motor and perceptual skills.

Research has found that sleep deprivation can affect our

ability to commit new things to memory as well as consolidate any new memories we create. That is why it is better for students to have a good night's rest before exams instead of going for all nighters.

The Stroop Effect is a phenomenon in which it is easier to say the colour of a word if it matches the semantic meaning of the word. For example, if someone asked you to say the colour of the word "black" that was also printed in black ink, it would be easier to say the correct colour than if it were printed in green ink. If, red is written in blue while orange is written in green, it will be confusing to name the colour.

As opposed to the above, the Priming Effect occurs when an individual's exposure to a certain stimulus subconsciously influences his or her response to a subsequent stimulus. These stimuli are often related to words or images that people see during their day-to-day lives. To fill in the missing letter in SO _P after seeing words like vegetables, cooking, or hot, we would automatically say SOUP. However, we would be inclined to say SOAP if we were to complete the word after words like bath, shower, water, etc!

Another interesting fact about our memory is its ability to associate a scent with a particular occurrence or event. It acts as a powerful memory trigger. In Rabindranath Tagore's poem "My Mother", the fragrance of shiuli flowers reminds him of his mother. A particular scent can bring forth a rush of vivid memories. The smell of rain or something cooking might remind us of spending time at our grandmother's house when we were small.

Smells have a stronger link to memory and emotion than any of the other senses. This is because the olfactory nerve is located very close to the amygdale, the area of the brain that is connected to the experience of emotion as well as emotional memory. In addition, the olfactory nerve is very close to the hippocampus, which is associated with memory. The actual ability to smell is highly linked to memory. Research has shown that when areas of the brain connected to memory are damaged, the ability to identify smells is actually impaired.

A popular notion about memory links aging with memory loss but it is actually erroneous. The memory loss people experience as they age is because they tend to exercise their brains less. Both physical activity, which increases the oxygen level to the brain and mental activity which stimulates synaptic connections in the neurons can ensure we continue to have good memories right into old age. For this, socializing and connecting with people are as important staying active.

These are some fascinating facts about our memories which make us realize with wonder how remarkable our brain is.

✧✧✧✧✧

## 3.4 Me and My Memory

### How Memory Works

Have you ever wondered how our brain works or whether it is possible to work on it? The movie *Ghajini* made us familiar with the term "Short Term Memory Loss", where the hero who had suffered a severe head injury, was unable to remember anything he saw or heard for more than a few seconds.

Short-term memory loss is caused not only by concussions and head trauma but also by lack of oxygen to the brain, alcohol and drug abuse and certain medical conditions such as seizures, epilepsy, heart bypass surgery and depression.

Short-term memory refers to the very short time that we keep something in mind before either dismissing it or transferring it to long-term memory. Basically, it holds a small amount of .information in an active, readily-available state for a short period of time. However, what we usually think of as "memory" in day-to-day usage, is actually long-term memory, but, there are also important short-term and sensory memory processes, which must be worked through before a long-term memory can be established.

Sensory Memory is the earliest stage of memory during which sensory information from the environment is stored for a very brief period of time. Paying attention to sensory memories ensures it passes into the next stage: short-term memory. Short-Term Memory is also known as working memory or active memory. It is the information we are currently aware of or thinking about. It refers to the processes that are used to temporarily store, organize, and manipulate information. In Freudian psychology, STM would be referred to as the conscious mind. Time and inattention may cause information stored in STM to be forgotten, but, paying attention allows it to continue to the next stage: long-term memory.

Long-Term Memory refers to the continuing storage of information. In LTM, information can be stored indefinitely and it also has immense storage capacity. In Freudian psychology, LTM would be called the pre-conscious and unconscious. This information is outside our awareness but can be called into working memory to be used when needed.

LTM can be categorized into different types of memories—declarative or procedural memory and explicit or implicit memory. Declarative memory ("knowing what") is memory of facts and past events, and refers to those memories that can be consciously recalled (or "declared") rather than performed. It is sometimes called explicit memory (Information you have to consciously work to remember). Procedural memory ("knowing how") is the unconscious memory of skills and how to do things such as tying a shoelace, playing a guitar or riding a bike. These memories are typically acquired through repetition and practice, and are so deeply embedded that we are no longer aware of them. It is sometimes referred to as implicit memory (information that you remember unconsciously and effortlessly)

After information is stored it needs to be retrieved to use it. Retrieval is the process through which stored information is accessed. While STM is retrieved in the order in which it is stored (e.g., a sequential list of numbers), LTM is retrieved through association (e.g., remembering where you parked your car by returning to the entrance through which you accessed a shopping mall)

The process, however, does not end when information is stored in Long Term Memory. Forgetting is a natural part of the learning process. One exposure to something new is usually not enough for long-term retention. Simple repetition works fine if we need to access information only for a short period of time, but elaborate rehearsal is more effective for creating Long-Term Memory. Research has found that approximately 56 per cent of information is forgotten within an hour, 66 per cent after a day, and 75 per cent after six days. However, with repeated and spaced retrieval of that information, learning will become more durable.

As we grow older, the length of time our short-term memory can store information becomes shorter. Also, our brains have less time to successfully move new information to long-term memory, making us more likely to forget details of recent events. Memory lapses and cognitive decline are a normal part of aging, but not an inevitable one, we can work to slow down the process by maintaining a brain-healthy lifestyle and keeping our memory active. Memories, or rather the neuro-pathways that are used to recall them, are strengthened each time we remember them. Actively practising recalling a memory, like studying for a test, will increase our brain's ability to remember. So, we can work to improve our memories.

✧✧✧✧✧

## 3.5 Cerebral Stuff

### *How to Improve Memory*

Scientists have been learning more about the brain's amazing capacity to change and grow new neural connections each day, even in old age. This flexibility and change that is constantly occurring in the brain is called **neuroplasticity**. We can harness the natural power of neuroplasticity to increase our cognitive abilities and improve our memory at any age. With the right stimulation, our brain can form new neural pathways, alter existing connections, and adapt and react in ever-changing ways.

Some of the research-proven strategies which can effectively improve memory, enhance recall, and increase retention of information are: Learning continuously, using all the senses, visualizing concepts, following a healthy behaviour, and meditating. A few of the best and time-tested methods have been enumerated below:

Going for higher educational qualifications is one of them. The adage 'use it or lose it' is true as much for memory as for other faculties. So, studying increases synaptic connections in the brain as, engaging in mentally stimulating activities sharpens the brain. We can stay mentally active also by being in a job or by pursuing a hobby or by learning a new language or learning to play a musical instrument. We must do something new that involves a skill we do not usually use and make lifelong learning a priority to enable building and preserving brain connections. Learning a new skill constantly challenges the brain and helps strengthen its memory capacity. We will have to find something that forces us out of our comfort zone and commands our full attention.

Paying attention to what we want to learn or remember is what will make the information move from the short term memory to the long term memory. It takes about eight seconds of intense focus to process a piece of information into our memory. Attention is one of the major components of memory.

Using the non-dominant hand is an interesting brain exercise that one neurobiologist says might help "keep our brain alive" and strengthen our mind. Because using our opposite hand can be so challenging, it can be a great way to increase brain activity. We could try switching hands while eating or when trying to write something down. New studies show that older adults who take up drawing instead of writing can improve on their memory, even though they are not good at it. It calls on more areas of the brain and forms synaptic connections. Besides, drawing can act as a therapeutic intervention to help hold on to valuable episodic memories.

Not only do brain-stimulating activities help the brain, even physical activity—walking and exercise fuel the brain as they increase blood circulation to the brain. While walking as such is good, getting out into nature or going for a walk in a park is far more beneficial to the brain and improves memory more than walking in the city as it also has a calming and refreshing effect. Similarly, gardening too lowers our risk of dementia. This is also because all our senses are involved where we can try to relate information to colours, textures, smells, and tastes.

We should try and challenge all senses when venturing into the unfamiliar For example we could try to guess the ingredients when smelling and tasting a new dish. We could give sculpting or ceramics a try, noting the feel and smell of the materials being used. The more senses we use while learning something new, the more the brain will be involved in retaining it. Not only should we study visually, but also repeat it out aloud, so that we are seeing as well as hearing the information. Even if one is a visual learner, reading out aloud helps to remember better. Writing it down is even more effective, as the physical act of rewriting information can help imprint it onto the brain. (Writing is thinking)

The mind plays a very important role in every aspect of our life, whether success in a venture or restoring ourselves to good health after being unwell. It is the same with memory too—If we believe we can improve and we translate that belief into practice, we have a better chance of keeping our mind sharp. Older learners do better when the messages about memory preservation into old age are positive while myths about aging can contribute to a failing memory. People who believe that they are in control of their memory function are more likely to work to maintain or improve their memory skills and therefore are more likely not to experience cognitive decline.

Spaced Learning as opposed to cramming is a better technique to follow while studying. It is designed to avoid the situation where the synapses become "maxed out" or lose their ability to learn new information. Having two separate study sessions, with time between the sessions, can result in twice the learning as a single study session of the same total time length. Students who study regularly remember the material far better than those who do all of their studying in one marathon session.

To remember something we have just heard, read, or thought about, we should repeat it out loudly or write it down. That way, we reinforce the memory or the connection created between the neurons. For example, using a person's name when we speak with him, saying loudly where we have placed our belongings if we have kept them at a place different from usual. Repetition is a potent learning tool. However, it is best not to repeat something many times in a short period. Like spaced learning, Spaced Rehearsal improves recall. However, Repetition and rehearsal are ineffective learning tools if used on their own. We will need to sit back later and actively try to retrieve the information without looking at where we wrote it down. Testing ourselves to retrieve the information is better than repeated studying. Practising retrieval creates more long-term and meaningful learning experiences.

Educators and psychologists have also discovered that when students actually teach new concepts to others and practise explaining the ideas to someone else in their own words, it enhances understanding and recall. The more often you share what you have learned, the stronger that information will become in your memory.—Steve Brunkhorst

For new data, we should connect (associate) it to the information we already know and remember—whether it's new material that builds on previous knowledge, or something as simple as an address of someone who lives on a street where we already know someone.

Association always aids in recalling and making mnemonics is a creative way to help us associate the information using clues to remember stuff.

a) Visual image—We associate a visual image with a word or name, for example, the name Surya Gayathri can be recalled by remembering the sun and a person chanting.

b) In Acrostics (or sentence), the first letter of each word represents the initial of what we want to remember. For example, the sentence "My Very Educated

Mother Just Served Us Nine (Pizzas)" can be used to memorize the names and sequence of the planets.

c) An Acronym is a word that is made up by taking the first letters of all the key words or ideas we need to remember and creating a new word out of them. For example, PAISA to remember the names of oceans-Pacific, Arctic, Indian, Southern (Antarctic), and Atlantic, RICE to remember first-aid advice for injured limbs: Rest, Ice, Compression, and Elevation.

d) Rhymes and alliteration (a repeating sound or syllable) are memorable ways to remember more mundane facts and figures. For example, the rhyme "Thirty days hath September, April, June, and November" can be used to remember the months of the year with only 30 days in them; similarly, facts like "i before e, except after c" and "In 1492, Columbus sailed the ocean blue."

e) Chunking breaks a long list of numbers or other types of information into smaller, more manageable chunks. For example, remembering a 10-digit phone number by breaking it down into three sets of numbers: 555-867-5309 (as opposed to 5558675309). Grouping—the individual digits 1, 9, 6, and 1 may be easier to remember by grouping them as the year 1961 and the digits 6, 2, 5, 4, 3, 9, and 1 might be more readily recalled as the telephone number 625-4391.

Sleep is one of the most important elements in having a good memory. Sleep is known as a memory enhancer by protecting memories from interfering stimuli. Taking a nap after learning something new can actually help us learn faster and remember better as the key memory-enhancing activity occurs during the deepest stages of sleep. Research shows that sleep is necessary for both memory consolidation as well as retrieval of information. Both quantity and quality of sleep are important to memory. To avoid sleep deprivation most of us need 7.5 to 9 hours of sleep every night. So, getting too little sleep or waking frequently at night can lead to fatigue which interferes with memory, creativity, problem-solving abilities, and critical thinking skills. So, a good night's rest is essential to ensure good memory.

When we think of ways to improve memory, we usually think of "serious" activities such as trying out difficult crossword puzzles or mastering chess strategy. Actually, light-hearted pastimes like hanging out with friends or enjoying a funny movie are more effective and even have cognitive benefits. *Healthy relationships are the ultimate brain boosters*. In fact, interacting with others may provide the best kind of brain exercise. Having meaningful friendships and a strong support system is vital not only to emotional health, but also to brain health. Even just ten minutes of talking to another person improves memory. Laughter is truly the best medicine as it engages multiple regions across the whole brain. It seems to help people think more broadly and associate more freely. Furthermore, listening to jokes and working out punch lines activate areas of the brain vital to learning and creativity. We should surround ourselves with reminders of our loved ones and us having fun and also spend time with fun, playful people. Not only should we observe the spontaneity of children but also learn to emulate them.

We know meditation is relaxing and soothing for our body and mind but, it is also good for our brain. It helps improve several cognitive functions like attention, focus, concentration, empathy, creativity, memory, and learning and reasoning skills. Meditation, with its power to help us concentrate, has also been shown to improve working memory abilities (short-term memory) after just two weeks.

Since our brain stops processing information as actively as it normally would during meditation, it relaxes the brain. Meditation also increases the thickness of the cerebral cortex and encourages more connections between brain cells—all of which increases mental sharpness and memory ability.

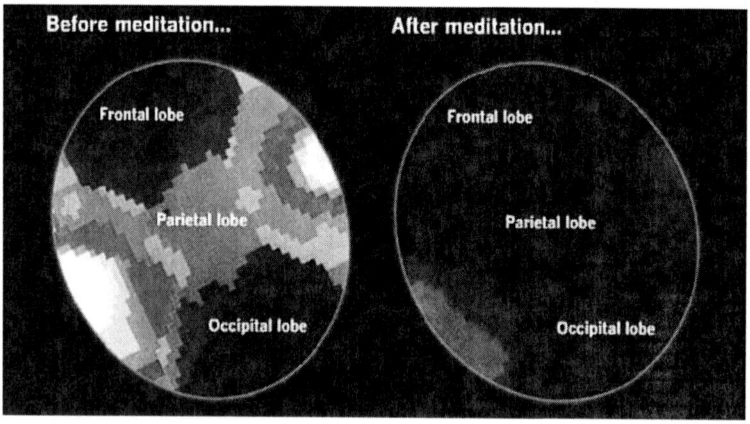


Having healthy food like plant-based foods, especially greens, fruits and vegetables, berries, nuts, legumes, coconut oil, herbs and spices, Omega 3's (walnuts, flax seeds, etc), Vit D supplement and plenty of water is good for the brain. For brain health, though, it is not just what we eat—it is also what we do not eat. Avoiding or having less of added sugar, carbohydrates, fried foods, salt, processed foods, cheese, etc is equally necessary.

Finally, to improve our memory, we should understand our own style of learning. Most people are visual learners, remembering best what they see. They benefit the most from memory notebooks and signs. Others are auditory learners, remembering best what they hear. They benefit from talking out loud or using a tape recorder. A few people are kinesthetic learners, remembering best what they experience. They will benefit most from writing things down or acting them out. Knowing our strength will help our memory run at peak efficiency. To enhance our memory, we should try using all three learning modes.

To sum up, we must read, write, challenge our mind daily, exercise, adopt a growth mindset (motivate ourselves, stay positive), meditate, spend time with friends and connect with people, go for walks, learn something new and stay active. Our memory is a skill, and just like other skills, it can be improved with practice and healthy overall habits.

✧✧✧✧✧

## 3.6 Purpose of Education

### Relevance of Universities

One may raise questions about the relevance of universities post COVID-19. We have been talking about online education replacing universities and digitalization fulfilling the requirements of the present education system in this age where online classes have become an important facet of learning. I would like to touch upon the purpose of a university and the intrinsic responsibilities attached to it. The views are drawn from the book, *'Building Universities That Matter"* by Pankaj Chandra. I have done this purely to motivate the stakeholders to work to fulfil the unsaid promised duties towards the students and towards society at large. Discussion is available at https://www.youtube.com/watch?v=W1nV7AJMxFo about the book and the thought process behind it.

When Dronacharya demanded that his 'disciple' Ekalavya give his thumb as Guru dakshina, one may think that he did that because he did not want anybody to be better than Arjuna. However, it is not convincing. Will a Guru be so cruel to his disciple? It makes me think that Dronacharya's thinking was much beyond our perception. He was definitely surprised with the mastery and the skill of Ekalavya. He knew that a person who learns skills and gains knowledge without the wisdom and the understanding which go with it to differentiate between right and wrong will be a disaster and largely be bad for society too. He realized that Ekalavya had learnt the art through devotion, but without proper mentoring and guidance from a Guru. Dronacharya knew that any learning without a Guru will never fulfil the purpose of education. He took his thumb so that Ekalavya would never use his art for a wrong purpose in life. In hindsight, we realize the astuteness of Guru Dronacharya as, Ekalavya later incurred the wrath of Shri Krishna when he tried to attack Dwaraka.

So, what is the purpose of education? The purpose education should accomplish is...

1. **Students should imbibe and fulfil constitutional obligations as good citizens.** The educated should show respect for the laws of the land and freedom of others, have high tolerance for diversity, listen to others' views, have a great desire for peace and co-existence and be generous towards those less endowed.

2. **Students must develop courage, compassion, fairness and a mindset to face challenges**. They should be agents of change for the future and motivate others to change.

3. **Prepare youth for livelihood.** Institutions must provide unlimited knowledge to enable students to think in new ways and focus on different ways of contributing to society. Stress should be not on just getting a job, but the right one which one is passionate about. Presently, the environment needs specialists rather than generalists. There is a need to focus on

the depth of contribution.

4. **Learning for Life.** Institutions must focus on and create in students a passion for learning, a lifelong quest for knowledge that one is seeking, a desire to draw one's own meaning in life and discover self.

5. **Guru-Shishya Relationship.** Members of the faculty should be seen not just as teachers, but also as facilitators, guides, mentors, role-models, enablers, counsellors—in fact everything. A Guru-shishya relationship is life-long and all encompassing. The teacher's role is not just teaching. It is not knowledge alone that is important, but putting it in perspective and providing insights on how to use it in practical life. Institutions, however, shrink in their actual purpose to simply preparing manpower for industry, that too of minimal quality, whereas, the main purpose of education is for the Guru to facilitate their students to develop a love for learning. You give a man a fish, he will eat it once but if you teach him how to catch a fish, he will eat lifelong. Institutions should teach the art of enabling one to succeed. In reality, there is wide gap between what we learn and what we do. There is lot of difference in what we want others to do and what we do.

   Thiruvalluvar said, "One should learn and learn well, without any fault. Then, one should implement the same in life without deviating from the correct method of what one has learnt."

6. **Way of life**. Institutions have to be a place of worship—a temple of learning. A place which is welcoming, warm, comforting as well as grooming and provides wisdom to get inspired, provokes

questions and answers, builds beliefs and destroys myths. It should become a way of life where one learns to live with others forming lifelong relationships, become skilled through diverse experiences and gain knowledge during the journey of academic discovery. As Rabindranath Tagore believed, there are many invisibles in the education in a university campus that shape the mind, heart and soul.

If that is the purpose, it is we, the stakeholders in the organization, who have to play our role properly. Our education must deliver INTEGRATED KNOWLEDGE, encourage students towards in-depth analysis in classrooms, guide students as to what to think and how to think, and develop healthy interaction between faculty members and students in and out of classrooms to develop all-round personalities.

It is said that higher education flourishes when you define the outcome and leave the choice of instruments to achieve excellence. For this, an institutional work-environment, freedom to think and work and empowering of the faculty to dedicatedly work towards educating students is required. Our tendency to place the accountability of the faculty towards the rules rather than on the outcome should be curtailed.

The environment of the institution should be ready for students to face the rigour of university education. The aim is to make good students into better students and not just average ones. The bonding between the student and the institution must be everlasting. As an alumnus, a student should feel free to fall back to the institution for any guidance and support. On their part, the alumni should be torch bearers to new batches of students and brand ambassadors to the institution and active participants in the growth and development of their Alma Mater. **A good institution builds its unique brand.** There is something unique in the students' conduct which stands out. The institution is recognized by the way its students handle their life situations. Ultimately, however, successful education is one which ensures a fulfilling and satisfying life, be it in whatever field one is in.

There is a requirement to innovate the best form of education in the existing circumstances; so, one cannot be far behind in the race. We have to be updated with developments, make room for the new and delete the old, the irrelevant and the outdated. We could go for a combination of classroom study, field study, online study, self study, research, institutional interactions and so on, that would give the best to the students. We must ensure that the form of education is very close to reality and is purpose-oriented. All work and no play make Jack a dull boy. Education encompasses indoor and outdoor activities, co-curricular activities, arts, drama, sports, social service, character development and so on. Peer interaction, competition, co-working are all part of the life in a campus.

Digitalization, distance learning, and online courses can be a supplement but ultimately education in a university cannot be overlooked. Universities are not built with cement and mortar alone, they are Temples of Education that mould the life of the youth—the university turns out to be a way of life. The faculty members are blessed people whose assigned duty is to transform the students into good citizens in society who fulfil the purpose of education in every way. This is something that no online courses can fulfil.

✧✧✧✧✧

## 3.7 The Course to Pursue

### Choosing College and Stream

We stand at the crossroads when school is over and the 'quantum leap' to college has to be made. There is a lucky minority that is able to decide the course/stream and the college well ahead in time. However, the vast majority of students and their parents are in a quandary and look for guidance.

This article aims to address these two issues—what are the key aspects to keep in mind while deciding a college and what are the trending courses that also have a bright future.

**Blended Mode of Education.** In the present age, post corona, online education has come to be accepted as normal. With online and offline modes of teaching or a blended approach to education coming into effective implementation, one cannot deny the fact that the university or the college you choose should be resourceful and technologically advanced. Proper connectivity to ensure continuity in online classes and a back up of sessions to refer to, are essential for the learning process.

**A Node for Knowledge.** Although one might prefer a college or university nearer home, we should not forget that the institution should primarily function as a 'node for knowledge'. This will provide you with the possibility of connecting with the required academic and information banks or knowledge repositories of the world. From such nodes you can also do certification courses from any institution in the world as per your choice and it may also facilitate exchange programs, dual degrees, etc., through the digital world. Digitally advanced and dynamic nodes are good to look for.

**An updated curriculum in sync with the environmental requirement.** A university must work with the times, with adequate updated curriculum in sync with the environment. A university or college with facilities like incubation centre, innovation labs, entrepreneur workshops and good internship should be preferred. This would add real value and also enhance placement opportunities.

**Members of faculty of high calibre.** The institution you choose must have a correct mix of experienced faculty members as well as newcomers. While you should not miss the experience and the experiential knowledge provided by seniors, you must equally have faculty members who are updated with the latest knowledge and trends and ready to adapt.

**Infrastructure both for Academic and Administration purposes.** The college or the university must be very spacious with all required facilities and amenities including administrative support like hostels, transport, canteen, etc. A university, which has good resources in both infrastructure and latest methods of teaching, will have an edge over others.

**Accessible Library.** A good library with the latest facility to connect you with e-learning and provide you e-books for reference is good. One should be able to use the resource through the net and have access to other sources as well as through a well developed digital library.

**Flexibility in Education and availability of multidisciplinary and liberal studies**. With the introduction of the New Education Policy (NEP), a university that can connect you well with traditional face-to-face learning using digital tools is better. The university which is adequately equipped with a wide range of subjects to include academic, vocational and non–academic, non-vocational subjects like NCC, music, sports, arts, community service, etc., should be preferred. This will provide an option for the student to choose/change and be flexible in terms of time and mode of learning. As of now, there are few colleges and universities with wide choices of courses under one umbrella.

**Role of institutions**. Institutions should be good facilitators to the students in the present environment where faculty members function more as coaches, mentors and guides to provide the best placement of their choice. University placement records will help you know the culture and effectiveness of the placement departments. Apart from this, one should not forget to get an idea about the teaching facilities available in the college. Good institutions are the ones which have facilities like MOOC, SWAYAM, Sim lab, FOSSEE, flipped classrooms, Blogging, sticky notes, shared documents and an advanced methodology of integrating resources with education for better understanding and research work.

**Modernization**. If you are not updated, then you are outdated. One should not compromise on quality of education for the cost-saving aspect. It is the parents' duty to facilitate their wards by ensuring correct availability of resources even at the cost of paying a little extra because, universities without facilities like library management servers, simulation-based virtual labs, reliable cloud computing facility and internet, studio with high HD camera, good lighting and proper effects and other supporting tools cannot expect their wards to cope with studies in the present advanced environment with a technology-dependent blended method of education.

**Look for all-round development.** The university or the college you choose should not only help in starting your own ventures and provide adequate entrepreneur training, it should also help you to develop an all-round personality. There are institutions which focus on this. They have a separate Learning and Development department to take care of this. In the 'T' type of development, while the vertical line represents the depth of knowledge that you acquire in your selected field, the horizontal line represents personality development. It requires no emphasis to say that equal focus should be given to the development of communication, emotional intelligence, aptitude, character, discipline and personality. Choose the one which pays attention to this. The institution must also have the wherewithal to provide adequate facilities for sports and entertainment. Also if you can get an institution that provides you with a cross-cultural (national and international) environment, then do not miss the opportunity if all your other criteria are met.

**Managing student pressure.** There are institutions that take personal care of students as far as their emotional health is concerned. They provide adequate emotional support to handle educational and other pressures. Some institutions do have qualified counsellors/therapists to provide emotional first aid, do interventions and help in finding solutions to handle stress. It is a place where students can vent their feelings. This will help both parents and the institution to monitor and correct issues of the students right at the beginning, instead of getting to know at a later point when they become non-reversible ones or lead to mishaps. Educating the mind without educating the heart is no education at all. So, do pay attention to this aspect while choosing a university for your child.

The second part of the question is what course should one opt for?

Education in present times is shifting to student-centric instead of teacher-based, giving importance to discovery, research and higher studies rather than to rote learning. Students should choose that branch which is of their choice and taste instead of sticking to fixed options of the yester years. No subject is inferior or superior; it is a matter of liking and passion. The present concept of flexible learning also helps you to experiment with multiple entries and exits, add credits of your choice to make the grade and get certificates or degrees at your pace. Multi-disciplinary education is becoming the order of the day (a concept of liberal studies). The student, at no point of time is forced to continue in the line selected. He has the option to make his grades depending upon his choice (even if he opts for a new stream later) the market and the environmental need. This is very essential in the existing fast-changing circumstances.

The choice of discipline or course should be based not only on one's interests, but also by looking into the future. Getting to know the present trends is important. As per the survey and report 2021 edition, (https://youtu.be/cEUJOEO-nCA), the 14 Growing Industries are Internet of Things, Artificial Intelligence, Cyber Security, Genomics, Drones, Robotics, Virtual Reality, Nano technology, renewable energy, sharing economy, e-learning, Big data, 3 D printing and Block chain technology. The interested student should go to Google and get to know more about the scope of his choice. Parents should encourage him to go ahead without fear with his chosen field by selecting the institution that has his required stream. He should select that institution which has the best accreditation, good culture, learning environment and is digitally advanced to effectively blend online learning with offline classes and uses virtual e-learning advanced methodologies to help him reach his goal.

So, one can consider all these important factors and choose the university which is updated to the present requirement as well as ready for the new changed scenario. Do select education centres that can cope with the requirement of educational needs in the digitised world.

✧✧✧✧✧

# CHAPTER 4

# ME & LEADERSHIP

## 4.1 Break Inertia

### I Make Small Fulfilling Resolutions

Leadership is not always about leading others; it is also about setting goals for oneself and achieving them.

Some time or the other, I am sure every one of us must have made a promise to fulfil a number of resolutions. Studies show that more than 80 per cent of resolutions are abandoned within a week or two. We can challenge our conscious self with our mind as to whether we stick to our resolutions. I bet, we will lose and our minds will win. Our mind, by nature, wishes for more but it is weak and gives up soon. Our mind does not want to change –The Law of Inertia is at work

It will resist change but the fact is that we do not grow without change. If we do not change, we become outdated and extinct. "One thing that is constant is change," said Heraclitus in 500 BC. Change should be welcomed. If we operate from our comfort zone, we fail to smell the cheese to know when it is getting old and to think that things are not changing is pure complacence. Be it anything, it is never static. Therefore, our development is based on our conviction in accepting change.

If we want to succeed, we have to be firm in our mind to change and be adaptable according to the need of the situation. Often we make a resolution without getting to know why we want it, what exactly we want and how we want to do it. If we have big resolutions, we are bound to get stuck at the first step. Let us ask ourselves, Can I do it? Is it very specific and clear? A mini step is better to start with. I recommend we should have one resolution at a time and not more. We can pick the next one after we make the first one a habit. We must ensure that our repeated habit performance is measurable and within our capability to achieve and remember that noticing small changes early encourages us to be ready for the bigger changes that are yet to come. When we work on our resolution, we must always see that our direction is result-oriented and time-bound. We have to be patient and be at it for 21 to 90 days depending upon what resolution we make. Only then can we make it an enjoyable habit.

In fact, we should word our resolution into a mission statement. For example, "I will walk for 45 minutes daily from 5 to 5.45 am. in the park for the next 90 days and reduce my weight by 1 Kg"

Here, it is specific, measurable, achievable (goal depends on individual ability, priority and purpose), result-oriented and time-bound.

We can write a mission statement after making a resolution by asking ourselves– what should I do? How should I do it? When should I do it?

Let me first fix the goal—what do I want to do? Improve my health or my communication skills or my listening habit? Ok, I choose health. If health, then again I should ask myself, which aspect in health? Reduce BP or control sugar or reduce weight or reduce the waist line? Say waist line. Then ask how? By walking or cycling or swimming? Finally, I arrive at reducing my waist line by walking. Then ask how much of waist line? I decide I want to reduce just half an inch and I may have the time and mind to do just half an hour or maybe only 15 minutes of walking. I can choose a park or a treadmill in the gym. I may prefer to do it only thrice or four times a week depending on my other commitments. However, all said and done, I have to make it a workable resolution. I have to first fix a mini target because I cannot afford to lose.

Once the statement is made, I have to put it in a place that hits my eye daily and reminds me of the commitment I have made to myself. I must also keep an auditor—my well-wisher—to remind/question me if I am sincere in my commitment and efforts. Still, if I find it difficult, then I must analyse my mission statement and make it still simpler—an achievable goal and start all over again.

I have to stick to my time-bound commitment. I must work at least for 21 days continuously and remember that if I stop in between, I have to start all over again till my goal is met.

Finally, whether I am part of a small successful group or of the majority procrastinating group depends on what I choose to believe and my determination. Achieving what I have set myself to do gives me confidence and makes me ready for bigger challenges. That is the stuff a leader is made of—to lead by example.

✧✧✧✧✧

## 4.2 Delegation

### A Leadership Style

It was in the late 70s; I was a young Lieutenant in the Army, posted in an Infantry battalion. One day, I was called by my Battalion Commander (CO), and asked to take charge of our basketball team and participate in the Inter-Battalion Basketball Tournament that would be held soon. Being a sports person and also good at the game, I organized the team and started our practice. My CO was a veteran at the game. He had represented the team at the services level in the early 60s. So, he was emotionally involved and wanted a definite win. Although he liked me as a good sportsman and knew that I could organize the game and motivate the team to win, he was not happy to know that his name was not included. Immediately, he changed the leader and gave the responsibility to my colleague. I became a player. Understanding the situation, my colleague did not make the same mistake of leaving out the CO's name from the team. The competition started. My CO occupied the central position and would expect everyone to pass the ball to him not realizing that he was in his 40s and playing with youngsters in their 20s. and that he was out of place. He would get angry and upset if the ball came fast on to him or if someone cut in between while picking it up or if the ball moved a little beyond his reach during a pass. He was fully blocked from throwing the ball in the basket and found it difficult to break through the opponent's defences. The CO was losing his stamina and started shouting at all of us as we were losing to the other team. It was half time when his colleague called him separately and told him, "You are good, but it is time for you to let go. And let go fully, don't control the execution—you have chosen the best team and given them the task. You are not expected to fight from the front. Trust and leave them to play their game." The CO withdrew from the team which was straining to charge! The energy of the team being high, the speed was tremendous and the second half was a win, win, win.

This brings me to highlight the aspect of Delegation. Most of us assume that we are the best for the jobs which we assign to our subordinates. We involuntarily get involved in the execution and start directing the team as to how to go about it. The team also, in order to operate from a comfort zone and not face a confrontation, welcomes the delegator, makes him feel good with all praises and thus entangles him in the work. The result, which obviously cannot be the best, is accepted because the leader himself is involved in it. A large number of external factors not under our control are listed as reasons for the failure.

What are the ways of delegation?

> **Complete.** As a leader, one must learn to let go. One must delegate or assign the task fully to the person or team, on whom he is 100 per cent sure. Let the delegation be clear—i.e., the purpose and the goals set to be achieved should be absolutely clear to all. After that, one should never control the execution. A good team will have a thousand options and ways to achieve the goal. All they require is the authority, the leader's support if something does not go as planned, the trust, the required resources to fulfil the goal and the required time to complete the task.
>
> **Indirect.** Again, this does not mean that one should take control of the execution. Here it is by monitoring of the task. Fix milestones to ensure that the assigned task is moving in the right direction. The leader can have a feedback loop system in case the assignments are difficult. Periodic reviews, reassessment of the goal, reframing the task and directing towards a new

goal to achieve the purpose are all the responsibility of the leader.

**Emergency**. When problems arise and the situation calls for emergency intervention, a leader may review the goal and the resources and change the approach of linear tasking to a multi-level approach or take control himself if necessary. The leader is always focused on the purpose and the short-term goals can be reframed to achieve the purpose.

**Central.** Should a leader exercise absolute control? No. Yet, the leader is always responsible. He has to have control, a functional control. Imagine that you are revolving a BOLA (a stone tied to the end of a string). The stone will rotate, if there is adequate tension force, enough to ensure that the rope does not slag and also does not break. There should be a right combination of the centripetal, centrifugal, gravitational forces and tension in the string which can keep the stone in position. Likewise, a leader must give adequate space to operate, not breathe down the necks of his subordinates, and yet, be available at the right time and place when required and be close enough to provide the right impetus.

**Responsibility and Accountability**. If the subordinate feels responsible for his task, then his performance will be of high-quality, he will take the initiative, be committed to his task, and find the right ways to ensure all things function properly. So, the leader is also relaxed and efficiency is more. On the contrary, if the person does not take responsibility, then there is ambiguity in the execution. Also, if the delegated person or team does not have an authority and reporting procedure, then he and his team will remain unaccountable and blame others. So, while delegating the task, remember whom you are delegating to, who he is reporting to & who he is responsible to. If A delegates a job to B and the responsibility is assigned to C, then B will blame D, E, and F for all delays, irresponsible work, and mistakes. So, one should ensure that there is clarity in assigning responsibility and proper accountability in the channel of reporting.

In short, delegation and responsibility should be very clear, direct, and accountable. Dual responsibility, lack of accountability, authority, and clarity are the reasons for non-completion of most of the tasks. Delegation is an art and science. The leader who knows how to delegate is calm and confident. He is like the conductor of an ORCHESTRA. He can orchestrate the tasks so well that simultaneously all actions run smoothly under the section principals and one hears only music and not sound.

✧✧✧✧✧

## 4.3 Problem Solving

### Root Cause Analysis

The movie *'Taare Zameen Par'* was a resounding blockbuster not just because of the actor Aamir Khan, or the songs which became great hits but also and mainly because of the story line—the theme—which was a path-breaking one in 2007. It deals with a child who is a dyslexic, but of which the parents are unaware. The child does not do well in school and is a constant source of frustration for the father and the teachers. The father believes his son Darsheel is bone lazy and finally decides much against the mother's wishes, to put him in a boarding school, feeling that the discipline there would have a better effect on him and he would improve academically. The child feels even more lonely and lost in the new environment. However, as good luck would have it, a new

Art Teacher bursts onto the scene and he infects the students with joy and enthusiasm. It is he who understands what exactly the stumbling block for Darsheel is and sets out to help him find himself. He helps him improve his reading and writing skills using remedial techniques developed by dyslexia specialists. He discovers the boy's hidden interest and talent in drawing and motivates him to participate in a drawing competition, in which Darsheel stands first in the whole school. So, the child who started out believing he was a total failure is totally transformed by the end of the story because of the caring and understanding art teacher who is able to address the actual problem and work towards resolving it.

That brings into focus the topic in question—'Problem Solving'. Steve Jobs' words ring true, "If you define the problem correctly, you almost have the solution." To do that, one must go to the core and tackle it, not the effect. Tackling the effect would only be cosmetic, whereas, probably what actually is required is surgery. "If I had an hour to solve a problem I'd spend 55 minutes thinking about and defining the problem and five minutes thinking about solutions." says Albert Einstein which puts in perspective how important it is to get an overall, broad, and deep picture rather than a narrow, myopic one. There is no point hacking at the leaves when we should actually be digging at the roots!

So, problem solving is not rushing to find a solution, as what we see may actually be only the tip of the iceberg. It requires first and foremost, an in-depth understanding of the problem and getting a grip of it. It involves data collection from multiple sources, and a detailed analysis. It necessitates looking at the issue rationally with an open mind and without a bias, thus getting to the root cause or the origin and finally framing the problem. Only after that are we in a position to start seeking a solution. This is generally called

ROOT CAUSE ANALYSIS (RCA). Wrong diagnosis will lead to wrong treatment and will have its undesirable effect.

A powerful tool for getting to the actual issue of the problem is by using a FISHBONE DIAGRAM. For example, misbehaviour by a student. It moves from the outer bigger set of bones to smallest ones at the narrow end. To get to the actual problem, one has to go to that smallest bone up to the end. In almost all cases, without exception, what starts as a small issue gets magnified many times and many fold by the time a decision to take action is arrived at. No matter what we address, unless this issue is resolved, the problem will only subside superficially and temporarily or have a negative outcome. However, if it is dealt with from the root cause we would not be faced with the crisis when it reaches gigantic proportions.

The poem we learnt in school, "For want of a Nail" brings this out very clearly. It is a popular rhyme dating back to the 14th century reminding us that seemingly unimportant acts or omissions can have grave and unforeseen consequences. The words of this meaningful poem, can teach us the simple fact that each of our actions, no matter how unimportant we think they are, will have an outcome and effect. "For want of a nail, the shoe was lost. For want of a shoe, the horse was lost. For want of a horse, the rider was lost. For want of a rider, the battle was lost. For want of a battle, the kingdom was lost. And all for the want of a horseshoe nail."

It shows that a major catastrophe can be traced back to a small error and the lack of a small object can lead from one unwanted consequence to another larger one to yet another one, as in a stack of falling dominos.

Atul Gawande, an Indian American endocrine surgeon, says this for doctors, but it is applicable for all when faced with a problem, "We always hope for the easy fix: the one simple change that will erase a problem in a stroke. However, few things in life work this way—success requires making a hundred small steps go right, one after the other, no slip-ups, no goofs, everyone pitching in." In most cases, however, we tend to fix the person than the problem with the result that we get involved in a blame game culture.

A quick fix remedy is similar to the allopathic mode of treatment, which is very important in serious and acute cases. We need it for immediate relief from suffering. In chronic, long-standing cases, going for the alternate mode of treatment would be more appropriate. To ensure the problem does not surface again after having been suppressed for a while, we will have to do an RCA and get to the root cause or origin of the issue and focus on that. "Successful problem solving requires finding the right solution to the right problem. We fail more often because we solve the wrong problem than because we get the wrong solution to the right problem."

Everyone faces problems. How we look at it—our positive attitude—will determine how we solve it. We should learn to think outside the box and not follow the herd. Anthony Robbins even goes a step further when he says, "Every problem is a gift, without problems we wouldn't GROW." So let us welcome them, be ready to attack them head on and thus resolve them instead of spending time and energy going around the problem. Getting to the root cause of a problem alone will ensure we find a complete solution to any problem.

✧✧✧✧✧

## 4.4 Organizational Motivation

### Trust and Self-Respect

An interesting case came up for analysis. It was a type of human audit in an organization. They wanted to know how to perk up the motivation level to ensure peak performance from all. The problem they faced was, in spite of the fact that the organization was rocketing towards growth and was giving salaries far better than most similar organizations, at individual level the motivation was not as high as expected.

The organization was looking for an excellent continuity in the process and was setting up its unique culture. However, when one looked below the veneer, though the organizational spirit looked high, individual motivation was wanting. Mostly, the feeling and commitment towards the organization was far from the desirable level. All were working but it was without heart and soul or complete involvement—just to get done with the job in hand, not go the extra mile. A good-looking engine with a drained battery! The battery needed charging. In such circumstances, unless we look below the carpet, read between the lines or understand the unsaid, one can not really get to the root cause of the problem to take remedial steps.

For our study, four important factors or pointers were taken, based on which an informed conclusion was drawn.

The first factor was the employees' salary. The second was their professional growth. The third was the employees' self-respect, esteem, and freedom to work. The last factor was transparency in the organization. The employees were asked to prioritize these important factors that directly affected their motivational level. Interestingly, the priority projected was totally different from what was anticipated when seen superficially.

The first factor salary, instead of being the topmost priority, took the fourth place for the middle level employees and the third place for the lower level employees! The second factor, the employees' professional growth, was marked at the third place for the middle level employees and fourth position for the lower/shop floor level employees. Transparency, the fourth factor, stood at second priority position and, on the top of the list came the employees' self-worth, esteem, and recognition/acknowledgement of the position they were holding.

The results when tabulated become a lot clearer:

| *Sr. No.* | *Factors* | *High & Middle Level Employees* | *Low Level Employees* |
|---|---|---|---|
| 1 | Salary | IV | III |
| 2 | Professional Growth | III | IV |
| 3 | Self-Respect | I | I |
| 4 | Organizational Transparency | II | II |

So, while the factors salary and professional growth showed minor variations in priority, there was no second thought as to what was top priority when it came to individual identity and esteem.

The following inferences were made based on the results collected.

> **Salary**—Though the take home pay was important, one thing that strikingly came out was that the employees had a fair idea of the capacity and ability of the organization to pay and that depended on the overall health of the organization. What concerned them more than what they earned was whether the organization was fair in ensuring that the salary and increments were not influenced by politics and wrong inputs from non-experts in the field and whatsApp culture due to which some were rewarded

unreasonably whereas, those who were silent workers and had contributed more were left out.

**Professional Growth**—The low level employees looked for growth more in terms of increment to meet inflation needs after a certain point of stagnation, while, those who were in the middle level especially, always worked to do better, looking for a good experience to enable themselves to be prepared for the next level.

**Organizational Transparency** refers to those areas in the system that must be open and known to the employees. An alignment is possible only when everyone in the system knows the goal or the purpose and policy—the vision and the mission. Leaders must be clear about what they had to do and the target to achieve. The organizational policy should be fair, transparent and not get changed often. Predictability, safety, and freedom to work in the environment are also important. Right efforts by an employee must be appreciated and the right person should get the credit. An open-door policy, open house system, and faith are very important.

**Self-respect**—Safety and security are no longer fundamental requirements compelling a person to accept anything just to earn for his family. In fact, for the present generation, acknowledgment of self-worth and the quality of life have become the basic needs in Maslow's hierarchy. These are what motivate him. Every man values his self pride and esteem. Even the lowest staff motivational level blooms if this factor is taken care of.

Based on the inputs and analysis, we came up with some important points to be considered to ensure the morale in the organization stays high. This will result in growth both for the individual as well as for the organization—they can grow together to achieve greater heights.

First and foremost, it does good to remember that it takes a lot of effort and time in building positive energy in an organization, which can happen only when there is synergy between the various parts involved. Behind every successful event there are many hearts and hands that have contributed. Recognizing, acknowledging and appreciating will act as a force multiplier. Regular meetings to brainstorm issues will bring out many points in the open. Reprimand, if required, should be one on one whereas praise should be wholehearted and in the open.

Next, it is better to get expert advice from the field/unit experts than from those who jump in with their inexperienced misleading inputs. Choosing the right person for the right job is mandatory to ensure satisfaction on the whole. To have a good team and overall growth, one could emulate this model from the Army—a person should be able to handle things one level higher or up to two levels lower at any point of time. While the first takes care of one's growth, the second takes care of the team motivation and faith building. For a ship to sail smoothly, every member of the crew should play his role and help his crew mate too when required.

An organization is like a concert. It requires a high level orchestrating of sounds from various instruments to achieve harmony and symphony. Even if one instrument is out of tune the outcome will be discordant and fall below standard. I remember that my boss in the Parachute Regiment used to say that even the Packers (the labourers who packed the parachutes) are to be respected and appreciated as they play an equally important role in our safe jump from the aircraft, that is, our success.

A need for fairness to all is important as, at the end of the day, people care more for their self respect, self esteem and quality of life. Quality of life in any organization refers to quality in the work place, quality in job, quality in environment, quality in role, quality in opportunity, quality in learning and also quality in rewards.

Without emphasizing too much on the importance of being empathetic, fair and recognizing every member of the team in an unbiased way, I leave it as food for thought for all to work out as to how they could do it. Also, remember that to be able to motivate, we have to be persuasive, and to be persuasive, we must be believable; to be believable, we must be credible and to be credible we must be truthful.

So, it finally boils down to the intention—whether or not it is genuine and truthful. The core is always understood however much it is covered with flowery or showy stuff. So, purpose and genuineness of heart will work wonders as far as motivation goes.

"To handle yourself, use your head; to handle others, use your heart."

✧✧✧✧✧

## 4.5 Inspire

### EEE

Probably you are wondering what the title 'EEE' of this article means!

Well! Let me clarify. We are not at the dentist's showing our sparkling white (?) teeth, nor posing for a photograph giving a bright 'say cheese' smile! We are not talking of the popular triple EEE—Electrical and Electronics Engineering degree either.

I will come to it, but, before that, I just want to start by saying—there are two kinds of work, which we take up for earning or otherwise. One is called a job where we are involved more with the system and the other is called a service which has more to do with people. The first kind would include most of the categories in the office with files, machinery, software, hard ware, etc. The services sector would include those in the HR, the administration dept, the hospitality department, teachers, etc. Even our mothers at home are part of this services department!

Whether one is in a job or in a service, the triple E philosophy holds good. The three E's here refer to a philosophy that I just discovered. It is certainly not new, but definitely needs to be reiterated repeatedly. In fact, this triple E philosophy is far more important than qualifications and degrees! This EEE stands for the philosophy of Energy, Enthusiasm and Empathy!

These are vital elements in our lives to give the life-graph an upward curve. Have you seen people around you with BOUNDLESS ENERGY and wondered what magic pill they might have taken? Actually, the source of their boundless energy is what is already inside them that gives them that energy and enthusiasm. Here is the secret of the energy and enthusiasm—It is the purpose, the meaning, the objective or the goal for which they are working.

We see it pulsating in ourselves too, when there is an occasion to get ready for, or a project to complete, or a function to organize or a festival to celebrate. That purpose pumps us up with new-found energy. We achieve so much in such a short time. Here again the secret is—we know what we are doing, why we are doing it and by when it has to be done. So, the task, target and time frame are all fixed which act as guiding principles for us. That propels us and there seems to be magic in the air, happiness spreads like wildfire and the task is completed on schedule, unsupervised and with no external prodding or coaxing/counselling.

We have seen the great leaders of the pre-Independence era—it was the common purpose and goal of freeing our Motherland from the clutches of foreign rule which made them work tirelessly, ready to face any hardship and surmount every challenge. So, when there is something defined and clear to which we can look forward to, it infuses us with energy and enthusiasm. The process of setting short-term goals and achieving them adds to the E- EFFECT, which is, in fact, "INFECTIOUS."

"The wearer of the shoe knows where it pinches" is an oft-repeated quote. But, that is where the third E—EMPATHY comes in. We must try to place ourselves in the other man's shoes to understand his difficulties, problems, hardships and challenges. Taking an elevated stand does not give us the right perspective. We must think and try to answer for ourselves, "Why is that person behaving in this manner? What could the reason be? How can I help him?"

"Empathy", the third E, makes life beautiful and I would like to add a fourth one, "Encouragement." Understanding the other person's requirements, empathizing with him, and encouraging him would go a long way in setting things right. One generally wants neither sympathy and pity nor unwarranted advice. Rather, one needs a strong shoulder to lean on, a concerned ear and a caring heart. Moral support goes a long way and so does understanding/realizing you can bank on someone, during challenging times. When a person facing some difficulty or undue stress knows there is someone to back him up and is perceptive of what he is going through, half the battle is won. Add to that a few words of encouragement, and the person is already on the road to getting better. Empathy and Encouragement can pull a man up from the lowest pit. First, you say, "I am with you, I realize what you are undergoing." and then, you give him features to look forward to and reasons to pull himself up and out from the dregs and you are sure to have achieved your aim.

The four E's in a person are what make him a great leader. His energy and enthusiasm seem to 'cling on' to the others as it were and his empathy and encouragement make them want to follow him, come what may. To these four E's, others get added automatically. These four E's are like magnets drawing other E's like Effort, Enterprise, Efficiency, Effectiveness, Excellence, Exuberance, Experience and Expertise.

We might as well start the days ahead not just with a triple E, but with all the E's encompassed!

✧✧✧✧✧

# CHAPTER 5

# MY LIFE LESSONS

## 5.1 Sustained Efforts

### *Lage Raho Munna Bhai*

Leh—beautiful Leh—the capital of Ladakh, (in erstwhile J&K) is a place worth visiting at least once in a lifetime. It may be barren, but there is something about the place which makes it unforgettable. My brother-in-law, who is in the Army, was posted in Leh a few years ago and had kept insisting on our visiting the place while he was there. It finally worked out and we actually enjoyed the stark beauty and barren rocky features of all shapes, sizes, textures and hues. There were no trees or vegetation on those mountains, only huge landmasses rising into the sky and covered with snow in the distance. The air there is rare and quite dry and it was chilling to the bone. What surprised us were the mountains and rocky features.

Unlike mountains which we have usually seen, what struck us was that, in many places, the enormous mountains and other natural features, all of them, were actually smooth and rounded and curved, not uneven, rough and irregular. It was certainly an unexpected sight! There were rocks in some places that were jagged, sharp and scary; there were others which were jagged on one side but rounded on the other! It really seemed magical—at the same time, we could see rocks which were sharp as knives, broken and uneven, and also rocks which were as smooth and curved as a bald man's head! They seemed so incongruous.

That's when our guide informed us that they had gone through the natural process of wind erosion which was the reason for their smooth and rounded characteristics. What we had studied in school we could see in front of our eyes – It was amazing! Not only was the scene breath-taking, it was also an eye-opener to nature's ways of working slowly but surely. It was a continuous process that went on steadily, constantly, continuously and unrelentingly.

Nature's slow and sure process is also visible in the course a river takes as it meanders through the mountains—cutting through rock and making a path for itself. This does not happen in a day but in thousands of years! This also results in those smooth, round and shiny pebbles which we used to love to collect as children!

Can we see life lessons for ourselves in these natural processes? Are they actually so natural? If so, what makes it so difficult for us to keep up with something we have begun? (From Nature—so natural and also something which should come to us automatically or naturally). No, it does not come to us automatically or naturally, at least for most of us. However, it is those that persisted, went on, kept at it unflinchingly, braving all the odds, not paying heed to all the questions, comments, criticisms, advice, discouragement, persistent dissuasion, and also overcoming their own laziness ,inertia, procrastinating tendencies, who finally made it to the goal. It is not easy but it is the only way to accomplish anything worthwhile. It is the grit, determination and strong willpower which can lead us to what we want. Any amount of wishful thinking cannot accomplish the task. As they say, "If wishes were horses, beggars would ride!" Only rigorous practice and unstinted hard work can lead us to the goal.

There is a *doha* (couplet) in Hindi which reiterates the same idea:

*Karath, karath Abhyas ke, Jadmahti hoth sujan*
*Rasri awath jath ke, sil par parath Nishan*

This is the story of a boy who is turned away by his Gurukul teacher as he could not study or understand anything. As the boy slowly and sadly walked back towards his home, he came across an old well in the forest. One side of it had a deep groove, formed by the rope which was used to draw water from the well. That was the point of awakening in him! If a delicate rope could cut through even hard rock by its constant moving over it and rubbing it while drawing water, then it was possible even for him to study and master the subject by constantly working on it. He went back to his Guru and prayed to be accepted again. He then rose to become one of India's greatest Sanskrit scholars. Through dedicated hard work and practice, even the impossible becomes possible!

Bruce Lee, the master of Chinese martial arts says, "Practice makes perfect. After a long time of practising, our work will become natural, skilful, swift and steady." And, we have to practise to that level of perfection to make it look effortless and natural. Whether it is a magician or an orator or a cricket player or a soldier, only the extra dedicated effort would make him the best in his field. Brian Tracy puts it like this, "Practise the philosophy of continuous improvement. Get a little bit better every single day."

Whoever has achieved anything worthwhile has done it

only by long hours of hard work. What they stress on is the necessity for continuity, and keeping at it. The world's greatest boxer, Mohammad Ali's story of how a puny boy turned into a heavy weight champion, is the stuff which reads almost like a fairy tale. However, fact is actually stranger than fiction. Whether it is dieting and losing weight or fasting or exercising or playing or reading or deciding to learn something new or to do something one has not done earlier, the only key to success is to GO ON AND ON, KEEP IT GOING and BE AT IT. Lage Raho! And, you will surely win.

✧✧✧✧✧

## *5.2 The Right Way*

### *E or M*

The focus of this article is E or M? Ends or Means? Is it only the result that is important, or are the means that we adopt to attain our goal, of any consequence? Or, does the end justify the means? Is it the Purpose or the Process? Mind or Method? Thought or Action? Rationale or Result? Motive or Outcome? Intention or Projection? Rita Stradling believes that "The means are inconsequential, only the ends matter" implying that, if the final result is as desired, then any means—right or wrong—used to achieve it would be excusable. For example, many people achieve power, position and wealth by adopting questionable or unethical methods, but they firmly believe that they are justified in doing so as long as they are able to achieve their aims—the end justifies the means. For instance, when prosecuting lawyers or investigators find it difficult to prove a person to be guilty of an offence or crime by using the due processes of law, they may resort to a trick or trap to lure the accused to reveal the truth. In such cases, using the wrong means may lead to the desired result, but it is still questionable as the method used is wrong. Is getting things done by hook or crook right? Can one beg, borrow or steal to achieve one's goals?

We are faced with this dilemma almost every day in our lives. Society has now made it an unwritten law that the ends are more important than the means. It is the result that finally speaks—what you do to achieve it is secondary. We observe this aspect in almost all fields, starting from the highest levels in politics to activities in our day-to-day life such as securing a seat out of turn in the train. This is the case in all societies, but somehow it has come to be accepted that it is more prevalent in the West where the end entirely justifies the means.

Here is an illustration which shows such blanket labelling is wrong. A Kenyan athlete, Abel Mutai, had almost reached the finish line of a race, but seeing the sign posts, he got confused and stopped, believing that he had completed the race. A Spanish athlete, Ivan Fernandez, who was right behind him, realized his confusion and instead of taking advantage of the situation, shouted to Abel to continue running. However, Abel did not understand Spanish, so, Ivan literally pushed Abel to victory. When Ivan was questioned as to why he had permitted the Kenyan athlete to win, he replied, "I didn't let him win; he was going to win anyway." His supporters felt that he had let go of a God-sent opportunity, to which he responded, "What would be the merit of my victory or the honour of that medal and what would my mom think if I had won by wrong means?"

Gandhiji too had rejected the duality between means and ends and had gone to the other extreme and stated that it is means, rather than ends, which is the basis of morals and ethics in our life. Although we can choose our goal, we do not have much control over it, as we cannot know before the work is done whether these objectives will be achieved or not. Only our effort and the method we use to accomplish our aim are in our control. Different modes of striving will cause different kinds of results to be obtained. (Not at the physical level, but on the higher moral plane).The rightness of the means resorted to reveal our core values and also our attitude. "For Gandhiji, the means were more important than the end. In fact, they meant everything. According to him, "As the means so the end."

Whatever the field, the HOW and WHY, the motive, the intent, the reason and the means employed are more important than WHAT we do or the end we are aiming for. Education and Medicine are two important pillars in society—one gives life while the other builds character and moulds children for shouldering future responsibilities. If we ensure we adhere to the core principles for which they were embarked upon, then the means and ends will be in harmony. So, when a person works according to his conscience, then the means he takes up will also definitely be upright. If, on the other hand, he keeps the outcome as the prime focus, then he may not give so much importance to the methods used to accomplish it, the results would be disastrous. So, the focal point has to be understood and realized within oneself only.

The other noble profession—the Armed Forces—fulfils a great duty towards society; they are the protectors of the nation, guarding its borders at the cost of risking their lives. They are not doing it to earn awards; they are doing their duty. In fact, in the Memorial in Kohima, the famous words, "Tell them of us that we gave our today for their tomorrow" brings out the actual credo which Army men stand for. For them, the nation always comes first, even before their own lives. That is why their martyrdom is called the supreme sacrifice. As the goal or end is to protect the nation and they do their duty as they should, the means and ends are in resonance and that itself gives a meaning and purpose to their life.

Like the men who guard our frontiers, let our aims also be high. Every work is noble and it is in our hands to ensure that its reputation remains unsullied by underhand means. Instead of just doing something because it has to be done, or indulging in short cuts or using compromising means, let us put our heart and soul into it and there will be a marked difference in the task completed by us and by others. Such is the mark of a person who is passionate about his work.

In any action, one should be very clear about the purpose—that is, why are we are doing what we are doing. If the answer is conscientiously convincing and noble, the end will automatically be good. Ends/ results are where we want to reach from our Purpose or why we are doing it. If we have a noble purpose and a clear answer as to what we want, the means will be correct. Thus, only when the end is noble, can the means be noble too. So the means justifies the end and not the other way.. We should not put the cart before the horse!

Let us not ponder on the examples of wrong means giving great results as they are only cases of winning a battle but not the war. One cannot go against the right course and keep succeeding indefinitely in life. Hence, if we take care of the means, the end will take care of itself. When the means are noble, so too will be the end. Similarly, if the end visualized is good, so, too should the means to reach it be.

This will give mental fulfilment which is what makes life worthwhile. This has to be instilled as a deep-seated core value right from the beginning. Good parenting followed by good mentoring by teachers during the formative stage, play an important role in moulding and grooming the younger generation. If the fundamentals are taken care of from the beginning, the rest will automatically follow.

✧✧✧✧✧

## 5.3 Patience, Faith and Gratitude

### Sabar, Yakeen, Shukar

There is a variety of cactus which grows just one inch in ten years whereas a species of bamboo grows 35 inches per day! Herbs grow within a few days but are seasonal; on the other hand, the oak tree takes years even to mature. Some plants are perennial, some flower once in 12 years, some flower only once in their lifetime while some bloom throughout the year!

Each is unique. We have to give the time required for them to mature, bloom and bear fruit. We cannot rush them. We have to remember that the mango grows only in summers whereas the banana is available through the year while peas are suited for a cold climate. It is a matter of waiting for the right time. Everything will happen exactly when it is supposed to happen. We can give it any name; however, we have to remember that the timing is always perfect, never early and never late but it needs a little patience (Sabar), lot of faith (Yakeen) and gratitude (Shukar), and it is worth the wait.

Sabar, Yakeen and Shukar encompass a single habit bundle. It is not a sequential behaviour but a simultaneous one. When you have patience there is an augmented effect if you have faith and gratitude with it. Similarly, when you have faith you must have patience and show gratitude and when you express gratitude for blessings received, then you would have included enough patience and faith. Each is an exponential factor to the other, and the effect is a force multiplier while the benefits are countless.

Some children are early bloomers and some late. However, each has something distinct and solely individual within him. So, comparing and judging a person early may not prove to be right in later years. Give him time, have faith and show gratitude (acceptance and approval) at every point of the development however small it may be. Only then can the individual actually reach his true potential. Patience is not only the ability to wait, but also the ability to keep a good attitude while waiting. An attitude of gratitude towards life fills us with happiness and a positive mind set. While we wait for the opportune moment to achieve our goal, practice and training with faith is essential.

The ad on the TV during the Tokyo 2020 Olympics held from 23 July to 8 August 2021 brought out how sportspersons who had to wait for a whole year wondering whether the Olympics would be held at all did not while away their time moping. Instead, they trained hard at home and on their terrace since the stadiums, grounds and gyms were closed during the pandemic. They believed they would get a chance to participate and ensured they were fully prepared for it when it came. They believed they had "gained" a year and could practise more. Their hard work paid off. In fact, all our Indian sportspersons surpassed themselves and brought in the biggest haul of medals in the last 40 years.

Mirabai Chanu fared badly at the Rio Olympics 2016, but, not letting that affect her, she clinched the silver medal in the 2020 Olympics in weight lifting by dint of sheer hard work which involved patient slogging and faith for five long years. The Indian Army too similarly started Mission Olympics 2020 with a focused mind to win a medal in athletics. It identified people with potential, employed and trained them. Subedar Niraj Chopra accomplished what he had been trained for by winning the GOLD in the 2020 Tokyo Olympics in javelin throw, the first ever by an Indian in field and track events. We bagged seven medals in all, which is the best performance for India in Olympic history.

This quality of accepting circumstances with patience,

while not letting go of our aim is a very important life lesson. Acceptance also involves gratitude as otherwise one would be complaining about the pandemic or something else. Add to that faith and trust in the larger reason behind things that happen and it is a sure shot formula for success. "Everything always happens for a reason, for experience or a lesson. Nothing is ever wasted as the soul is gaining insight."

There are many examples from real life to illustrate how people have used patience, faith and gratitude in their lives to reach where they have reached. One is the story of the South African President and Nobel Peace Prize winner Nelson Mandela. His negotiations in the early 1990s with the South African President F.W. de Klerk helped end the country's apartheid system of racial segregation and ushered in a peaceful transition to majority rule. In April 1994 the Mandela-led ANC (African National Congress) won South Africa's first elections and he was sworn in as president of the country's first multi-ethnic government.

Once, as president, he went with his escort to a restaurant for lunch. There was a man at the next table waiting to be served. Mandela asked his soldier to ask him to join them. He sat next to Mandela but kept his head down, did not utter a word and his hands were constantly shaking while eating.

After they had finished, he said goodbye and left. The soldier was surprised and expressed that he must have been unwell as his hands were trembling. Nelson Mandela said, "No, not at all! The reason is something else. He was the warden of the prison where I stayed. He tortured me and did not even give me water when I pleaded for it. Instead, he laughed and humiliated me. Now, he is not ill, but scared that I will send him to jail and treat him the in the same way. But, I am not like that. This type of conduct is not part of my character or ethics. Minds that seek revenge destroy states while those that seek reconciliation build nations. Walking out of prison to freedom, I knew that if I did not leave behind all the anger, hatred and resentment, I would still be a prisoner." What noble thoughts! What high values and principles! Starting in 1952, he was severely restricted in travel, association and speech but, he did not become bitter. Despite being in prison for more than twenty years since 1964, he still had faith in his dream of ending the inequitable laws and apartheid policies. He did not behave in an unbecoming manner with the jailer who had ill-treated him. He did not hold any grudge against him or anyone else for imprisoning him for so long. He left behind the negative emotions in the prison when he walked out and instead carried positive thoughts of faith in his dream and in humanity. He was at peace with himself and his world—a goal he achieved purely because he had imbibed "Sabar, Yakeen and Shukar."

Another story of faith and patience is the how a single woman created a beautiful daffodil garden along the mountain slopes in California, all by herself. It is a glorious sight—there are five acres of flowers! The woman had begun more than fifty years earlier in 1958, one bulb at a time, year after year to bring her vision of beauty and joy to an obscure mountaintop and now there were more than 50,000 bulbs! The unknown woman had forever changed the world in which she lived. She had created something of extraordinary magnificence, beauty and inspiration.

The principle that her daffodil garden teaches is one of the greatest principles of celebration—learning to move towards our goals and desires one step at a time, with patience, faith and gratitude. When we multiply tiny pieces of time with small increments of daily effort, we too will find we can accomplish magnificent things. We can actually be the change that changes the world.

✧✧✧✧✧

## 5.4 It Is I

### Looking Inwards

There's a well-known quote, which goes like this: "God, grant me the serenity to accept the things I cannot change, courage to change the things I can, and wisdom to know the difference." There are many things in life, in fact, most things, which have to be accepted as they are. It is for us to change our mode of operation to move from mere coping to winning. The art of life lies in a constant readjustment to our surroundings.

Wherever we are, whether at home or at our place of work or any other place, if there is anything that does not match our thinking or view point, immediately, our hackles are raised and we start looking for who or what caused it. We tend to externalize the problem. It is as if, instead of standing in front of the mirror (called me) and seeing myself, I tend to look through a glass (called ego) outside me. I pick up many issues from outside, forgetting the hidden weaknesses within me and blame them on that over which I have no control. In reality, the environment will never adjust with me; it is I, who have to adapt myself with the environment. In fact, when things around me are not to my liking, I have two options. One is to not accept the things and react by quitting, which is a passive approach and requires no effort or fighting which is a negative approach and causes ill feeling all around. The other, more difficult option, but proactive approach is to accept the circumstances that are beyond me and ask myself what I should/can do about it and then, looking inward, respond by taking action befitting the situation or environment and still achieve what I have set out to do.

In both cases, the external environment has nothing to do with me in particular. It exists as it is and is not made especially for me. I too have no control over the external aspect. If I am able to think and analyse, I will realize that whatever happens—the events, the situation, the behaviour of people, in fact 95 per cent of everything around me is beyond my control. The only thing over which I have any control is over myself.

Epictetus is of the view that all things external are outside our control and should be accepted calmly and dispassionately. He reiterates, "Things in our control are opinion, pursuit, desire, aversion and whatever are our own actions." In fact, he declares, "It's not what happens to you but how you react to it that matters."

To quote from the *Geeta*, Lord Krishna says, "Whatever actions are performed by a man under any circumstance, he gets the fruits of those actions regardless of the circumstances." Therefore, let us not be obsessed with the environment and circumstances. It is our actions which are within our domain or, over which we have power and that alone matters.

This second option of working through the environment is difficult, as we have to win over our ego, the worst enemy that creates anger in us and prevents us from changing, adjusting and adapting to the circumstances without compromising on our core values, our ethics and our goal. Our worst enemy is anger/ego and the worst disease is covetousness.

(Yaksha: *What is the invincible enemy of men? What is their permanent disease*? Yudhishtra: *Anger is the most invincible enemy. Covetousness is the incurable disease.*)

Take for example the simplest of situations. If you have planned to go out, and it suddenly starts pouring, what can you do? There are so many things you can do—blame the weather and start fuming and ranting or you can see the sudden change in the situation and take an informed decision. Firstly, you can be grateful that you did not get caught in the rain and now prepare for it. You could take an umbrella or raincoat or you could take a car, or you could even decide not to step out and wait till the rain abates. There is one more option, and that might be to just go out despite the rain and enjoy the downpour in a childlike manner! All these options and decisions have to come from within, given the external situation, which has to be accepted as such.

We will realise that even when we can take decisions, many things are beyond our domain. Suppose I want to buy a house, yes, I do have the freedom to choose the locality, the budget, the type of interiors, the colour of the wall, etc. However, having bought the house can I choose my neighbour? Then what do I do? Either I learn to live amicably and adjust or sell my house and shift somewhere else. I may say that I will make him vacate, but once again I have to adjust with the new neighbour. Finally, it is always that 5 per cent (me) on which I have control. Similarly, while one has the liberty to choose one's job what comes as a package along with it are the boss, colleagues and subordinates! On a lighter note, we have the freedom to choose our spouse, but not our in-laws. It's a buy-one-get-two free situation!

Instead of finding fault and being dissatisfied with our lot, learning to look inward and taking the right action in the new environment shows prudence and wisdom. John Wooden says, "Adaptability is being able to adjust to any situation at any given time." and Max McKeon believes, "All failure is failure to adapt and all success is successful adaptation."

For becoming adaptable, we have to conquer the ego within us, adjust ourselves to the new setting and work to fit into the changed milieu. *Being able to adapt is actually a sign of higher intelligence.* Fighting, finding fault, not fitting in do not really show maturity in behaviour or consideration for the other person, whereas adapting ourselves to the new set of conditions reveals a lot more patience, presence of mind, flexibility and good sense. It is easy to fight and break away, but more difficult to *become a team member and yet not let go of our individuality*. Life is always a game of give and take. Rigidity does not serve the purpose or solve the problem whereas with flexibility and adaptability a lot more can be achieved.

All this points to us—to me—not the external environment. I must work to understand the situation and respond to it, not react. I should ask myself, "What should I do, what can I do under the existing scenario?"

We are responsible for our actions, but not for things around us which are not in our control. Looking inwards to see how to respond and act in the present circumstances alone is in our hands. Life is a constant struggle but, with self-discipline, confidence, sincere efforts and a 'can do attitude', we can achieve our aim. Learning to always see "what I can do in this situation" is a proactive approach. Looking inwards, not outwards, is the motto to happiness, success and good relationships. "I am responsible for my behaviour and no external circumstance can change that."

✧✧✧✧✧

## 5.5 Embrace Monotony Too

### Is Boredom Good?

(*Written during the first wave of corona*)

Once upon a time, in a far far away land, we led a different life. It almost seems that we are a distant alter-ego of our former selves. Well, sorry to be so dramatic! I am sure you will agree that our life has changed drastically during the corona period. We have changed, adjusted, adapted to the

New Normal. Life is not the same as it used to be.

I recall some of the conversations I have had with my students and fellow faculty members. All of us had felt that the schedule was highly demanding. There was too much pressure and time was not enough. Both personal and professional expectations and demands had made our lives a constant check list of tasks, a high-strung move from home to college and back. We desperately wanted time off. We wanted quality time with family, to read new books, to learn new skills and engage ourselves in activities that are more meaningful and have time for something more than the daily routine. And then, COVID-19 hit us like a tornado! We should have rejoiced that our prayers had been answered in an unexpected way. However, locked up indoors for months on end, it was a case of jumping from the frying pan into the fire! Life earlier seemed better; at least it was not dull. Now there is neither excitement nor anything to keep us engaged and busy and we feel like we are being dragged down by the monotony.

This is a universal phenomenon. Boredom is not unusual at work, especially when there is repetitiveness as in a factory, and it is linked to productivity loss and burnout. This becomes a serious concern for personal and professional well-being. Often children at school too experience boredom. Students get bored both when the topic is tough and they are not able to absorb it or when it is not challenging enough to prod them to think. And, bored students become dull and are restless without a way to channelize their energy. Boredom affects quality of learning and grades. In fact, there is a strong feeling that boredom leads to anti-social activities, destructive behaviour, getting into wrong company and habits to while away time, and sometimes indulging in perverted activities to get immediate gratification.

We notice that generally boredom leads to something

of the mouse or the flick of the remote or a touch of the smart screen, boredom has become more the norm than an exception. So, what can we do to deal with boredom? Can boredom be useful? What is the reason for boredom? What are the changes that we can make to ensure that our life is more productive and fulfilling? Here are a few quick tips to break through boredom:

- Set a simple and achievable yet challenging target for ourselves and also add a time limit to raise the bar further.

- Have Variety. When a level of saturation or satiation seems to be seeping in, we should change the activity. This not only relaxes us; it also helps us to concentrate better and increase interest simultaneously.

- Go for an adaptive approach to the action and outcome. When things do not go the way we desire, there is a tendency to avoid and repulse than adapt and accept. *A mind that accepts what it gets and redefines the short-term targets to improve further will make things interesting*. This will take us away from the practice of going in for easy gratification for escaping from the challenges by indulging in smoking, drinking, caffeine, surfing the net or even excessive sleeping to reduce the feeling of boredom.

- Embrace boredom. Let us think, feel and behave differently in a situation when we feel bored. Often, routine life and boring tasks make us reflect upon and ponder over our life. Let us spend that time on some introspection and creativity. It is an opportunity to reflect on ourselves and make plans on how to improve the situation. Boredom often drains us of our energy. When we introspect or think creatively or do something for the first time or do the same thing but in a different way, we feel energized.

Dr. Sandi Mann has come up with the theory that boredom has its benefits. She is a senior psychology lecturer at the University of Lancashire in the UK and has authored a book on this—*"The Upside of Downtime: Why Boredom is good."* She asks us to accept the emotion for what it is. It seems to be negative whereas it is actually a search for that something, which seems to be missing. It is necessary to acknowledge it and allow the brain to look for a meaningful solution. The mind plays an important role in this.

Trying to recollect and connect with the generation of the yester years, what would they have done when grinding flour or doing threshing and winnowing? It would have been a monotonous job but they did not seem to mind it. They would have done it as a community activity where a group of people joined hands to help each other out, which would have reduced the tedium of the work. At the same time, they would have talked and laughed and shared their thoughts with one another, which would have acted as a vent for them.

As a counterpart in the present high-tech world, our mobile phone has seemingly come to our rescue. Does it not furnish us with data and stimuli that we are constantly getting updates? Here is the flip side: It actually overloads us with information and so we live in a rarefied bubble where we do not feel bored while we are with the mobile. In reality, *we miss out on our emotional and social side of our life* which is very important—the main ingredient which took care of our previous generations. We also lack the opportunity to introspect and be creative.

According to Sandi Mann, the phone is actually neither letting us get bored nor properly entertaining us. So, there has to be a 'No mobile or other electronic gadgets time' in our daily routine.

Research says that we can benefit from the feeling of boredom. The next time when standing in a line or waiting indefinitely for the doctor or in a weary meeting, let us not turn to our mobile or plug in to a music app. That is the time when instead of moping due to boredom, we could try some introspection, or creative reflection. Our overall performance might improve.

The mind is a strong force behind everything that goes on. When we are getting bored doing the same work again and again or not enjoying what we are doing, *we require to pause, introspect and direct a new course or method to win over the boredom*. We could also try to bring in some newness in the routine and make it enjoyable—it is for us to find out how to do it. "If you are killing time, you are killing yourself."

Agreed, life needs variety to keep it beautiful. So, let us think of that which will add spice to life and work on it. Ups and downs in life, as in an ECG report, are what make it worthwhile. Boredom or stimulation is finally in the thinking. In fact, routine is the normal course which life takes and that itself gives it sanity, rather, there is a sense of comfort in the routine. Lockdown or restrictions and curbs, on-line or off-line, life has to go on positively and we can change our boredom to something that rejuvenates us. It is within us to find the way for it.

> *"Monotony is the law of nature.*
> *Look at the monotonous manner in which the sun rises.*
> *The monotony of necessary occupation is exhilarating and life giving."*
>
> —**Mahatma Gandhi**

✧✧✧✧✧

## 5.6 Ikigai

### A Reason for Being

I recently finished reading this book—IKIGAI (The Japanese secret to a Long and Happy life), and I'm not exaggerating when I say it is literally life changing. This book is very well written, and it explains problems that I'm sure all of us face today. In today's materialistic and stressful world, it can be very difficult to find our 'IKIGAI'—our reason to get out of bed every morning, something that makes us happy. There are people in this world, who are over a hundred years old and who are active and happy and do what they love! If they can be so passionate at their age, why not us!

This book teaches many lessons regarding how to nurture our friendships and how to overcome our personal fears and anxieties in order to lead a fulfilling life. A particular quote from the book that has struck a chord with me is—*'Being aware of the impermanence of things does not have to make us sad; it should help us love the present and those who surround us.'* This is a very important lesson, because there are certain things in life we cannot change, no matter how hard we try, and we have to learn to be happy despite them. If we let the past control us, and worry about the future, it will destroy us. The present is the most important time of all, and we have to focus on it. Even if we have not found something we are passionate about, it is okay. It will take time, but we will find it. Once we find our IKIGAI, the wait will have been worth it. The simplest things are often the most beautiful, and this book gives the perfect example for this statement. 'Eat right, exercise, and do what makes you happy'...by following this motto, we can definitely find our 'IKIGAI', our reason to live.

Steve Jobs himself was a big fan of Japanese design in porcelain and electronics. The spirit of "sophisticated simplicity" (in contrast to "lazy simplicity") is visible in Japanese art, engineering and cuisine. "The Japanese are skilled at bringing nature and technology together; not man versus nature, but rather a union of the two." In an era of urban stress and social media distraction, IKIGAI sheds light on the importance of focus, social ties, a healthy lifestyle, and a larger sense of purpose.

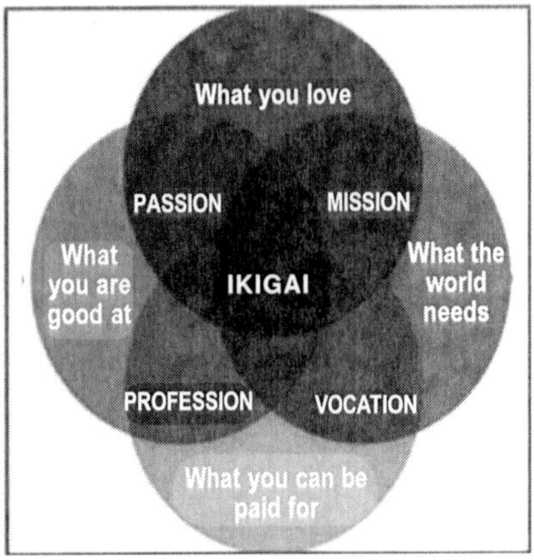


IKGAI translates into "the happiness of always being busy." In the Venn diagram, this "existential fuel" lies at the intersection of what you love, what you are good at, what you can be paid for, and what the world needs. It is unique for everyone and can change in the course of life.

In that sense, IKIGAI is much more than a passion or profession. This framework would make for great discussion on topics like social entrepreneurship. *If one has a sense of purpose in life, the concept of retirement does not matter.* Perspectives can be reset by examining the present from a future state and contrasting the present context with the worst-case scenarios. It is important to accept feelings of anxiety, fear, or worry; however, one should not succumb to them or even try to eliminate them.

The book brings out a number of important lessons for

us—People who live the longest have a positive mindset and a high degree of emotional awareness. They can manage their emotions during times of setbacks. While meditation "slows down the centrifuge" of the mind, mindfulness increases peace of mind and helps appreciate the more important as well as the finer aspects of life. A strong sense of humour and smiling at people (even strangers) helps. A low level of pressure and occasional stress may be beneficial, but continuous stress is physically harmful and can cause fatigue, depression, irritability, insomnia, and anxiety. Stoicism helps control distractions of pleasure and desire, through balance rather than elimination. A strong sense of resilience helps us overcome hurdles and also helps us to be flexible to adapt and switch tactics. (Acknowledge what cannot be changed). A very important aspect is to protect one's space and time to harness IKIGAI; a certain level of privacy and even reclusiveness is evident among many successful people.

Another very valuable point is the **concept of flow**, which psychologist Mihaly Csikszentmihalyi defines as "the state in which people are so involved in an activity that nothing else seems to matter; the experience itself is so enjoyable that people will do it at great cost, for the sheer sake of doing it." A sufficient level of challenge sustains the immersive power of flow; too much leads to anxiety, too little leads to boredom. Taking small steps at a time and cultivating a habit of discipline helps get past inertia blocks into the zone of flow.

A strong ability to focus and concentrate is called for to sustain flow; unplugging from digital media ("technology fasting") too helps here. Too much multi-tasking and interruption can lead to mistakes, wastage of time, reduced productivity, exhaustion, feeling of loss of control, less creativity, and inability to remember what was done. Routine activities and mundane tasks have an associated "micro flow"—for example, Bill Gates says he enjoys washing the dishes at night since it relaxes and clears his mind. Rituals also have their own aspects of flow and help break down big goals into sub-parts. "The happiest people in the world are not the ones who achieve the most. They are the ones who spend more time than others in a state of flow."

A number of studies in the book have focused on the lifestyles of centenarians from Okinawa and other 'Blue Zones' of the world where people live the longest, such as Sardinia, Loma Linda, Nicoya and Ikaria. They not only live fulfilling long lives but also suffer from fewer chronic illnesses and enjoy higher levels of vitality. We can learn from the fascinating insights of these people such as "Have a tremendous thirst for life" (Misao Okawa, 117); "I've never eaten meat in my life" (Maria Capovilla, 116); "I see badly, I hear badly, but everything's fine" (Jeanne Clement, 122); "Keep your mind and body busy" (Walter Breuning, 114) and "I haven't died yet" (Alexander Imich, 111).

The people of Okinawa have a strong sense of community, and celebrate the rituals of life. The 100 interviewed residents of Okinawa share a number of lessons: stay active, spend time with people, nurture friendships, cultivate a garden, eat healthy, smile, do regular exercise, have tea together, slow down, enjoy the little things, be optimistic, do volunteer work, indulge in laughter, song and dance, be grateful for each day and live in the moment. These are great lessons to imbibe and follow.

✧✧✧✧✧

# CHAPTER 6

# I AM THE CAPTAIN OF MY LIFE

## 6.1 My Thinking

### It's My Way of Life

Do you follow cricket? I wish to tell you the tale of two interesting characters on the cricket field—one is the critical and fault finding commentator and the other is the ever-supportive wicketkeeper who keeps shouting words of encouragement to the bowler and the fielders. Each one of us also has a Critical Commentator and a Supportive Wicketkeeper living deep down inside us. They give us thoughts and these thoughts shape our lives. It is these thoughts that create our actions, well-being, energy and perceptions. They form our life. It is not what we achieve in life but how we perceive our achievements that makes a difference. *Being satisfied, emotionally balanced and physically healthy are the outcomes of our positive thoughts to a large extent.*

As per our body science, every thought releases brain chemicals. Being occupied with negative thoughts saps the brain of its positive forcefulness, slows it down and can go as far as dimming our brain's ability to function, even creating depression. On the other hand, thinking positively and having happy, hopeful, optimistic, joyful thoughts changes the physiological conditions thereby decreasing Cortisol—a depressing agent and produces Serotonin which creates a sense of well being.

Most of the time we address the symptoms without addressing the root cause. For example to handle stress, we must address the cause that triggers it. Taking out anger on someone, brooding, etc., are not the answer to handle stress. When under stress, drinking a glass of water or doing yoga will only temporarily relax us but will never take us out of the problem. Suppose I am under stress due to examination fear, the cause for the same can be due to not properly preparing for it or not understanding the subject or may be something else. If you know the root cause, say in this case "Not understanding the subject", then is it not better to join a good coaching centre and learn the subject? Devote adequate time in search of a good tutor who can make you understand the subject better. For this, will not planning ahead relieve the stress before the exams?

It is one's perception that decides whether a situation is an opportunity or an obstacle. The time we look at a situation as an opportunity, the brain will work to find solutions to make things possible and if we think otherwise, the brain will give all justifications to convince us as to why it is a no go. It is said that everything will align the way one thinks.

Therefore develop positive thinking. Even "Impossible" can be read as "I'm Possible"

**Food for Thought:** *"Thought Power"* by Swami Sivananda is a simple, straightforward, inspiring book that holds many secrets on how to nurture thought power. It also presents useful suggestions to reach a region beyond the terrain of thought and its power, a realm of transcendental Experience and God-consciousness.

## 6.2 Churning

### Manthan

> *"The most beautiful people we have known are those who have known defeat, known suffering, known struggle, known loss, and have found their way out of the depths. These persons have an appreciation, sensitivity, and an understanding of life that fills them with compassion, gentleness, and a deep loving concern. Beautiful people do not just happen."*
>
> —**Elisabeth Kübler-Ross**

This quote reminded me of a story narrated by a scholarly lady when she wove a beautiful tapestry, connecting mythology with real life as she recounted the anecdote of the churning of the ocean of milk from the Bhagvad Puranas. It is the story of how the devas (gods) finally defeated the asuras (demons) and became immortal. She spoke of how the churning had first thrown up a poison (swallowed by Lord Shiva to stop it from spreading) and then it threw up a variety of treasures and finally came up the nectar of immortality—Amrita. As an analogy, in life too, she said, a lot of churning takes place and it is only after a lot of effort can we hope to reach a higher plane.

All of us are repositories of qualities both good and bad—there is love, but also covetousness and resentment. There is protectiveness along with jealousy. There is trust, but also anger, compassion, laziness, energy, greed, restraint, sorrow, happiness, kindliness, and sympathy along with callousness and heartlessness! In fact, we are all a concoction of opposite and conflicting qualities, some manifesting at one time and the other later. Our nature usually hovers between the two limits but sometimes, in rare cases, it swings like a pendulum from one extreme to the other—animalistic-humanistic-devilish-divine-selfish-selfless and generous,—a desire to destroy, harm or hurt but at the same time a desire to create, protect and comfort. There are books and movies that project the marked and contradictory qualities in an individual who is then labelled as a schizophrenic.

I would not like to go the extreme cases where such incongruous qualities are manifested in a very distinct and obvious manner. Rather, I want to emphasize the fact that these differing characteristics and qualities are natural in a human being, and it is in the course of life that we are able to grow away from negative traits and adopt the positive ones to become better human beings. Kobe Bryant rightly states, "Everything negative—pressure, challenges—is all an opportunity for me to rise."

Initially, as children, we crave everything for ourselves and tend to hoard things; we are selfish and do not want to share, we are possessive and want all affection and praise to be showered only on us. However, as we grow older and more mature, we realize the value of sharing with others—whether it is materialistic possessions or human qualities like love, honour, harmony and camaraderie. We move from giving prominence to ourselves as individuals to a higher level of becoming a team member. We learn to contribute for the growth of the team as a whole. We are able to move from competition to cooperation and collaboration. We progress from I to We and, from personal to universal. In addition, when a person is able to share his knowledge with others, so that they are also able to develop and grow, there is overall betterment in the society and community.

When an individual is able to bond well with others and work productively as a team member, we can say he has matured. The reason why sports is given so much importance is because it develops these qualities—there, it is not individual capability alone but the combined efforts of all the team members working towards a common goal which can give a win. Moreover, sports emphasizes more on whole-hearted participation than on winning. In fact, all are winners.

There is a South African term UBUNTU that means humanitarian spirit. It advocates a philosophical approach to life that emphasizes social unity and generosity of spirit, fellow feeling and kindness. It loosely translates to "I am, because we are", meaning to say we are interdependent and harmony is essential for coexistence. There is the story of a race for 'special children'. The story goes that one child slipped and fell halfway through the race. All the other children stopped, went back and picked up their friend and holding their hands together, reached the victory line as one team. The entire gathering of spectators rose in unison and gave a standing ovation. *It was a celebration of the human spirit, not of an individual.* The children might not have been mentally as "advanced" as others their age, but they were far more advanced as far as compassion, concern and consideration are concerned.

That is what is more important in life. Some people are able to reach that level early, but for most people it is a lifelong process of churning and being faced with hardships. As in the mythological story of the churning of the ocean of milk, initially, our bad qualities are manifested. Then come better ones, which help us stay comfortably in society with a healthy give and take and pleasant behaviour. Children throw tantrums, but, adults rarely do so. If a person behaves in an unbecoming fashion, we call him immature and his behaviour childish. When life throws up challenges in the early stages, it is the instinctive reaction inherited from our ancestors of either fight or flight that is displayed. However, instead of reacting, as we grow older, we learn to respond and resort to methods that would help in resolving the issue more amicably. We try to look at things from the other person's point of view and try to be more empathetic. So, from instinctive behaviour—at gut level—we move to a reasoning one where we begin to use our head and still later, use our heart to reach out to the other person.

The churning process finally brings out the best in us and we are able to feel the change within ourselves. That is the mark of a matured person. So, it is expected that a person, as he matures, will exhibit more humane qualities—be more generous in his dealings with others, be glad to share his knowledge, take life as it comes, be more open and willing to help others, etc.

I remember how as a young child, I used to watch with fascination as my grandmother used a wooden plunger (*manthan*) with a string wound around it to churn out butter from buttermilk, pulling the string back and forth with both hands to agitate the liquid. All of a sudden the soft, creamy, tasty homemade butter would be floating on top of the buttermilk and we used to vie with each other to have it! What I did not realize then was that there was actually a life lesson in it for all of us! The churning we go through in life brings out the best within us after initially throwing up unwanted/ superfluous stuff. After eliminating all the unnecessary and imbalanced qualities, we are sure to turn into pure and polished solid gold, from which all impurities have been removed. As Martha Graham would say, "Fire is the test of gold; adversity, of strong men." It also made me understand one more aspect. Whether in the case of the home-made butter using the *manthan* or in the mythological story, till the final required product came up—butter in the first case and nectar of immortality (*Amritha*) in the second, the person or people doing the churning, did not stop. That also means we must not give up on others or ourselves. If the final elevated state has not yet been achieved, it only means more churning, that is, going through more hardships and more difficulties will be required to reach that level. En route, a number of relatively insignificant or not so important advantages will be gained, like the treasures that came up when the ocean of milk was churned but, they continued till *Amritha* was finally obtained. So, too should we. It is only after going through all the adversities and difficulties of life that the best in us will finally emerge. The final goal should be kept in mind; we must not get carried away with wayside obstacles or advantages.

> *"And once the storm is over, you won't remember how you made it through, how you managed to survive. You won't even be sure, whether the storm is really over. But one thing is certain. When you come out of the storm, you won't be the same person who walked in. That's what this storm's all about."*
>
> —**Haruki Murakami**

✧✧✧✧✧

## 6.3 My Thought Power

### Mind Control

When I am doing any routine work, so many thoughts keep coming up in my mind, sometimes some jumping ahead of the others, so much so that I can almost hear an internal conversation going on! Why does this happen and does it happen with everybody? I tried to find out and was literally overwhelmed with terms like thoughts, perceptions, decisions, actions, self, conscious, unconscious, mind, brain, mood, behaviour, and concentration!

This is what I finally learnt—we believe that the mind keeps creating thoughts, but, in fact, it is not the mind that creates thoughts. It only holds them—it neither creates nor directly controls them. *It is the brain that creates thoughts, which then fill the mind*. Thoughts filled in the mind lead to perceptions, that is, how we see, understand and form an opinion on something. They direct us to make our decision, which is then followed by the required action.

Thus, our actions are a result of our thoughts and perceptions. We feel that we perceive things correctly; however, in reality, we make lots of mistakes. All of us know the story of the loyal mongoose on which the lady threw a basket of vegetables killing it only to later realize that she had totally misunderstood the scene. Seeing the mongoose with bloodstains and remembering that she had left her child alone at home, she was totally convinced that it had harmed her child and so, was a completely untrustworthy animal. However, it was too late when she realized that the mongoose had actually saved her child from a snake.

It is the brain at work here giving rise to wrong thoughts. In response to our senses, (to see, hear, taste, smell and feel), the brain quickly generates thoughts which then fill the mind that lead to perceptions. The thoughts originating from the brain depend on the way in which our brain network and the neurons in it operate, *influenced by previous experiences, bias, opinion, mindset, proximity, pattern and similarity*. So, there is a tendency for our decisions and actions to be prejudiced. It is said that as a response to our feelings (senses) there is always a coherent impulse in-built in us to encourage us to do things that promote our own survival. In fact, our brain always focuses on things that matter to us, but they may not actually be right. The interesting part is that these activities are not governed by our conscious self. Most of the times we feel that we are taking decisions but we seldom realize that *it is the unconscious inputs from the brain that drive the mind to take decisions*.

This necessitates the understanding of our brains. The brain has nerve cells or neurons which when activated, generate thoughts. The nerve network exists as bundles/ modules. Each module addresses one type of behavioural challenge. Douglas Kernik says, "Modern science talks of seven modules in our brain." These are also called the sub-selves. These modules are not in rigid compartments or localized. They are dynamic and in a continuous state of activity and they interact and communicate, expand and shrink depending on which factor is predominant at that moment. *These seven modules are naturally developed nerve bundles to respond to seven types of behaviours of a person*. These are self-protection, mate attraction, mate retention, affiliation, kin care, status, and disease avoidance. In accordance with that module which is activated most powerfully, the brain network empowers the respective organ to prepare to face the challenge. So, most of the decisions depend upon the way the modules work. So at a particular time, the decision depends on the modules/module which dominate/s. It is also called mood. About this Michal Gazzanija says, "It is a dog eat dog world, going on in your brain with different systems competing to make it to the surface to win this prize of conscious recognition. Whichever notion you happened to be conscious of at a particular moment, the same one comes bubbling up and that one becomes dominant."

In a particular mood, say self-protection, the decisions that flow to our mind will be to face and ensure self-protection and hence the self-protection module dominates. For example, a person who has seen or faced violence just prior to hearing even a neutral statement from another person is now in a self-protection behavioural challenge mood. He feels threatened or attacked and behaves in a defensive manner or even aggressively because his self-protection module is dominating at that point of time. Similarly, the advertising world also uses this **dominating factor technique** and works on the mind by creating thoughts in the brain, which make us, favour one product over another. This is because the bias influences the corresponding module to get activated due to repeated inputs to the brain through branding and media.

We know that the thoughts created by the module dominant in the brain have power over our mind. The instructions from the dominant module for each response fill the mind as thoughts. Does the mind have any role to play in the creation of thoughts? Yes. It can influence the brain. Actually, *the mind (which is abstract) holds the reins of the brain (concrete) having the seven modules.* An agitated or negative mind will influence the brain to produce wrong thoughts whereas a positive mind will ensure positive thoughts are created. The mind is like the jockey who controls the chariot or the brain from which arise the nerve bundles or modules. These modules are like galloping horses generating thoughts, which continuously fill the mind and when the mind fails to control the brain, the horses will gallop at free will. So, right thoughts are not generated to fill the mind, thus leading to wrong perceptions and actions.. On the other hand, if the thoughts from the brain are controlled by the mind like a good jockey using reins, the thoughts will not run haywire. Therefore, we have to train our minds and, in turn, our brains to think the right thoughts.

Can we train our minds? Yes, it can be done firstly by realizing and being aware that *the mind can be trained to control our brain*. The knowledge that efforts can achieve MIND POWER itself empowers us. Secondly, we can train our minds by practicing **mindfulness** and **concentration**. We can work to achieve mindfulness (a mental state reached by focusing one's awareness on the present moment) through **meditation** and **muscle relaxation** techniques, which help to finally calm the brain. This will make the brain relaxed and composed. An image of the brain taken when the mind is over-active and agitated will show the neurons all charged up and a lot of electro-chemical activity going on.* However, if the image is taken when the mind is calm, there will be minimum activity noticeable in the brain. Such an undisturbed condition can lead to the **right state of mind** (calmness, compassion, balanced way of thinking, right attitude and self-control), **concentration** and **focus**. Thirdly, the mind can give **positive reinforcements** to the brain by filtering out unwanted inputs and feeding in positive inputs repeatedly from the environment. Thus, when the mind ensures mindfulness (i.e., being Here and Now), and supplies positive reinforcements with focus and concentration, correct thoughts will be generated that will lead to right perception and action.

This is what Modern Psychology talks about. Unless our mind controls the brain and maintains a right state, the thoughts that are generated by the modules in the brain cannot lead to right perceptions, judgments or actions. The way to attain right mindfulness is by **meditation, concentration** and **positive reinforcement.** With this, Mind Power is activated and it can control the brain. In addition, with that, even the body can achieve what the mind believes as it is a case of *mind over matter*.

This is not a new philosophy. It is old wine packed in a new bottle. If you go back to the *Bhagawat Gita*, Krishna, represents the mind, the horses represent the seven nerve modules of our brain, the reins are the controls in the hands of a safe driver, Krishna, and the No man's land of the battlefield which belongs to neither the good (Pandavas) or the evil (Kauravas) represents a balanced mind, neutrality

*See page 73.

and calmness. These help Arjuna (self) to perceive life rightly and do the right actions.

✧✧✧✧✧

## 6.4 I am an Achiever

### Fly High

**If we do not achieve what we are capable of, then we are living below what we were created for. It is the greatest sin to be an under-achiever.**

There's the story of a man who finds an eagle's egg and places it in the nest of a backyard hen, along with the brood of hatching chickens. The baby eagle grows with the chickens, doing what they do. It pokes around in the dirt looking for worms. It flutters around at low levels and settles on the ground after a short flight. It clucks and flaps its wings with the chickens and scurries away when disturbed. Once, when it was quite old, it looked up and saw a majestic eagle flying at a great height, swooping down and then soaring up again. It glided ever so smoothly and looked regal and magnificent. He asked "What is that?" One of the chickens responded "Oh, that, that is an eagle. He is the king of the birds. He is the master of the skies. You don't bother yourself with that. We can't fly so high, we are meant to be on the ground." This eagle did not know about his original nature and **inner potential** and sighed in sorrow, "If only I could also fly high like that eagle." He lived and died believing he was a chicken, meant to spend his life with the flock of hens and chicks, confined to the ground, eating seeds, grains and worms!

That bird (the eagle), of all the birds he was among, had the desire to fly high, that *spark was within him*, not in any of the other birds. Yet, he accepted the condition he was in and did not even try to fly like the eagle in the sky. If only he had tried, he would have discovered his potential which was locked within him and did not have an opportunity to emerge. Thomas Jefferson rightly states, "If you want something you've never had, you must be willing to do something you've never done." So, if the eagle wished to glide in the skies, he would have to **break free from his mind, which** was conditioned to living on the ground with and like the chickens. It happens in the lives of so many people. Many of us live our lives like the deluded and sadly mistaken eagle, not realizing our inner potential and capabilities. We live like chickens on the ground when actually we should be flying high like the majestic eagle. Only some, sensing the spark within them, try something different and achieve their purpose. Most often, those around us may not be aware of our abilities, but sometimes we remain ignorant of our own aptitude and potential. Why does this happen?

This takes me to the fourth quadrant of the Johari window, the Dark Area or the unknown self. This area is the one that generally remains unexplored until our death. We fail to move out of our comfort zone mostly because of Fear, a psychological state of mind, often called xenophobia—a fear of the unknown (FOTU). It is harmful and impedes our growth. So, we have to come out of our comfort zone and grapple with our fear. Otherwise, our life will always remain incomplete. We can conquer fear by *visualizing and practising mindfulness, changing our perception and looking at it as a challenge to overcome.* We should stretch beyond our limits and take calculated risks. FEAR should mean—**Face Everything And Rise** and **not Forget Everything And Run**. Unless we explore, experiment and try, we will stagnate and not live a meaningful life. Only with grit and determination can we break through and overcome all obstacles like a fragile plant bursts out from a crack in a cemented structure.

### *The Johari Window*

| | ***What I know about myself*** | ***What I don't know about myself*** |
|---|---|---|
| ***What others know about me*** | **1. OPEN AREA** What a person knows about themselves and is known by others in the group or team | **2. BLIND SPOT** What a person does not know about themselves but which others know |
| ***What others don't know about me*** | **3. FAÇADE** What a person knows about themselves but others do not know | **4. UNKNOWN** What is unknown by the person about themselves and is unknown by others |

Take the case of Kalpana Chawla, who was born in Karnal, Haryana, in 1962. She was the first woman of Indian origin to go into space. In her village, girls' education was considered a luxury; yet her mother made sure that all her girls went to school. Always a passionate and confident child with lots of natural curiosity, she loved to discover how things worked. The sky, with stars twinkling in it, caught her fancy. She became interested in airplanes early in her childhood. In drawing classes, while her classmates drew mountains and rivers she would draw colourful airplanes and make airplane models in craft classes. Later, when in DAV College, while explaining the concept of null set in algebra, her teacher gave the example of Indian women astronauts as there was no Indian woman astronaut at that time. To everybody's surprise, Kalpana got up to say, "Who knows Ma'am, one day this set may not be empty!" She became an astronaut in NASA and a part of its space mission. She was able to realize her dreams. She did not just think or imagine or desire something unattainable, she also worked so hard that she made it achievable.

Our former President, Dr. A.P.J. Abdul Kalam firmly believed that, "We are all born with a divine fire in us. Our efforts should be to give wings to this fire and fill the world with the glow of its goodness." He is also known to have said, "If you want to shine like a sun, first burn like a sun."

How long are we going to take to make that decision of not living like chickens because conditions placed us there but live like the eagles that we were born to be? How long to make the shift? That requires introspection, SWOT analysis, courage, determined resolution and character. **Character** is the ability to carry out a resolution long after the excitement of the moment has passed. It is easy to start something, especially when everyone is making New Year resolutions. However, the ability to carry on with it and the ability to carry it to its fulfilment long after the initial thrill and hype die down, long after all the aching muscles tell you to stop or at least take a break is what speaks of character. It requires the courage of conviction and the power of resolve.

If we go back on the word given to ourselves, to the commitment made with ourselves and do not achieve what we are capable of, then we are living below what we were created for. It is the greatest sin to be an under-achiever. Sin is not used here in the religious sense. The word 'sin' comes from the Greek word 'Hamartia' used in archery meaning "to miss your mark'. Typically, most persons perceive sin to be something that one should not do, rather than *the failure to do something positive*, which is implied in "missing the mark." Hamartia implies that we have a target and perhaps even a place on that target that we are trying to hit! The greatest sin on earth is to miss our mark—to be under-achievers, to not accomplish what we were meant to, to fall short of our capabilities, to not be who we were created to be—to be a chicken instead of an eagle.

Let us remember Dr. Abdul Kalam's words, reiterating the above thoughts, "Small Aim is a crime." and make a new beginning—aim high and attain great heights. Let us all make new LIFE Resolutions and become the eagles we were born to be.

✧✧✧✧✧

## 6.5 Finis

### My Goal in Life

**The end crowns the work:**
**The goal gives value to the labour that produced it.**

The old man said, "It does not have the finish."

I was taken aback. I had done the job as required and could see nothing left out. Then what did he mean? Bewildered, I asked, "May I know what that means?"

The old man smiled and replied. "It is not completing the job—it is the finis that includes the final goal/purpose for which you did the job.

"For example, you have joined a college...a good college...you studied well...and got a good grade."

"But, is it finished with that? No. You might have won the first battle but there is lot more to do to win the war. What it means is that each step takes us nearer our goal. Completing a degree or Master's or even a PhD are only the means to the end."

In the case above, ask yourself whether the purpose was to get a grade or a degree or something else? Is your vision accomplished?"

"Ask yourself repeatedly...'why' and 'so what' till you get no further answer. Maybe, then you will be close to your purpose or vision. The purpose is the end or the goal. For example, in this case you may identify a purpose like...I want to be the best civil engineer to ensure that I provide affordable houses to all. The job is finished only at that point when you fulfil that purpose. Mere successful completion of your degree means nothing beyond holding an approved qualification. You have to work beyond your education to get to your purpose or goal."

The old man elaborated, "The Latin word 'finis' has two meanings: the end or the finish, and a goal to reach. The second meaning—a goal to reach is what I am referring to. So, when I initially expressed that your work does not have a finis, what I meant was that you have **to strive to find the inner purpose for doing this and see if you have achieved it**. A man who cannot see the end, that is, purpose of his "provisional existence" will not be able to aim to reach the vision or the ultimate goal in life"

"One must have a clear vision. The tasks you perform en route to reach your goal are just the steps you take to reach the target or the rungs of the ladder you climb to get to the top. Most of us perform tasks without identifying the vision or core aim and without a goal to attain. A task completed implies that the task is over, but it may be without the finer finis."

A classic example is the Afghan crisis in which the Taliban took over Afghanistan. Pakistan supported the Taliban hardliners and the TTP and was bent on establishing a government of its choice and they pulled it off. However, did they achieve their goal? No! The job is just over but it is not finished. Now starts the challenge for Pakistan. Will it be able to sustain the bankruptcy and support an isolated Afghanistan? Can it handle the humanitarian and social challenges in Afghanistan spilling out of the current situation? If the vision of Pakistan was to have a friendly and stable neighbour, then how are they going to address the internal and external turmoil, Baluchistan and the offshoot problems of terrorism in Pakistan? Can they ensure a safe Durand Line to keep the borders calm? The job is done, but the goal is not achieved and not finished. That's it."

You are born, live your period and then die. You have lived your life. But in reality your life gets over without a finis. A good finis is only when the purpose of your life is fulfilled. You may say, I did well, earned well and enjoyed with a lot of money and power. However, if you ask...Why do you want the money and power? The question remains unanswered. One may say, I wanted to be happy and I got it but tell me if there is any person who does not want to be happy? Is that a purpose? Happiness is an outcome of achieving the purpose that you set for yourself. Money and power are some tools to fulfil the purpose. If you have lived a life without a purpose then it is without a finish. *Finding the purpose of our life sometimes takes a lifetime and the search must go on till it is found.* Once you hit upon it, it becomes easier to work for the goal or purpose. Finding the purpose is the key to living our life in the best possible way.

Suppose, I set my purpose to be a good facilitator to help the youth and enable them to become good human beings in society. I find that this purpose can be achieved by becoming a good teacher or professor. I work hard towards the field of my choosing, to become eligible and competent to take up the responsibility of a Guru or a mentor/facilitator.

During this journey, I reform the education system benefitting all and I am able to produce a number of students who are capable, good, self-dependent, confident and purposeful citizens. Now my purpose is achieved and I have the sense of having a good finis when I retire. So, the fulfilment of a Vision is different from completion of tasks and work.

So, let us try to have a great finis in every endeavour we start than simply completing it.

✧✧✧✧✧

# AFTERWORD

The process of putting together and compiling the various articles, clubbing similar ones under a suitable chapter, narrowing down on and choosing a title for the book, the headings for the chapters and finally doing the proof reading has been an enjoyable one.

Hope your journey down the pages was not only a pleasant one but also useful. If it has prodded you to think and evaluate your life and has been a guide and helped to steer your future course, the aim of this book would have been achieved.

The authors of this book wish you a happy, purposeful and fulfilling life.

Thank you for being with us.

✧✧✧✧✧